BUSINESS STRATEGY

OTHER ECONOMIST BOOKS

Guide to Analysing Companies
Guide to Business Modelling
Guide to Business Planning
Guide to Economic Indicators
Guide to the European Union
Guide to Management Ideas
Numbers Guide
Style Guide

Dictionary of Business
Dictionary of Economics
International Dictionary of Finance

Brands and Branding
Business Consulting
Business Ethics
Business Miscellany
China's Stockmarket
Dealing with Financial Risk
Future of Technology
Globalisation
Guide to Financial Markets
Headhunters and How to Use Them
Successful Mergers
The City
Wall Street

Essential Director
Essential Economics
Essential Finance
Essential Internet
Essential Investment
Essential Negotiation

Pocket World in Figures

BUSINESS STRATEGY

A Guide to Effective Decision-Making

Jeremy Kourdi

THE ECONOMIST IN ASSOCIATION WITH
PROFILE BOOKS LTD

Published by Profile Books Ltd
3A Exmouth House, Pine Street, London EC1R OJH
www.profilebooks.com

Typeset in EcoType by MacGuru Ltd
info@macguru.org.uk

Printed and bound in Great Britain by Clays, Bungay, Suffolk

A CIP catalogue record for this book is available
from the British Library

ISBN-10: 1 86197 459 0
ISBN-13: 978 1 86197 459 4

The paper this book is printed on is certified by the © 1996 Forest Stewardship
Council A.C. (FSC). It is ancient-forest friendly. The printer holds FSC chain of
custody SGS-COC-2061

FSC
Mixed Sources
Product group from well-managed
forests and other controlled sources

Cert no. SGS-COC-2061
www.fsc.org
© 1996 Forest Stewardship Council

Contents

Introduction

The essence of the ultimate decision remains impenetrable to the observer – often, indeed, to the decider himself ... There will always be the dark and tangled stretches in the decision-making process – mysterious to even those who may be intimately involved.

John F. Kennedy, former American president

Strategic decisions are rarely straightforward or simple. This is because they involve value judgments that depend to a large degree on people's attitudes, perceptions and assumptions. This is why so many strategic decisions turn out to be ill-judged.

The aim of this book is to help those who have to make strategic decisions and to throw light on the decision-making process. The first part focuses on the forces shaping major decisions, including ideas, developments and potential pitfalls. The second part outlines practical insights and techniques for handling decisions. Some of these ideas are tried and trusted. Others, such as information orientation and reversal theory, are recently developed approaches providing valuable techniques and guidance for leaders.

Strategic decisions are the choices that determine the direction and success of organisations. Although many strategic decision-makers are senior managers, entrepreneurs and leaders, increasingly those lower down the management structure are being empowered with the responsibility for making strategic decisions. This is because organisations are flatter and more customer-centric than ever before, driven by the forces of change and complexity that are greater and faster moving than ever.

Although it makes sense to move decision-making closer to where it has its impact, the extent to which decision-making spreads through an organisation and the techniques applied vary from sector to sector. For example, legal firms are often conservative and hierarchical, dominated by the nature of their profession, whereas software firms are typically characterised by "bottom-up" rather than "top-down" management, reflecting the challenges and culture of their industry. What matters is how individual organisations make decisions and implement them relative to their competitors. It follows that there is no single approach to strategic decision-making to fit every situation, organisation or person.

There are, however, broad truths and techniques for strategic decision-makers, and these are explored in this book.

It is said that experience is valuable only as long as the future resembles the past. Superficially, this may appear true, but in truth, experience is valuable even if the future does not resemble the past because it helps us to understand and cope with change and the unknown. It is not simply what we know that matters, but how we react to what we do not know. How we do is influenced greatly by our experience. The art of strategic decision-making lies in both how we react to what we do not know and how we react to clearly defined situations.

There are techniques that can prepare managers to cope with the unknown, enabling them to ride the waves of change and drive their organisations forward. Such techniques are examined in the second section of this book. Experience points the way to likely futures, where new situations or "rules" are emerging. These will shape the way that we work and develop organisations in the future.

By understanding the forces that shape decisions in organisations today or which will become part of the management agenda in the future, we are better able to understand the context for strategic decision-making. Coming up with ideas and solutions that are rooted in the experiences and behaviours of the past is of limited value. What matters more is an appreciation of the forces shaping business strategy, the ideas influencing decisions and the pitfalls of strategic thinking, resulting in more effective strategic decisions.

1
THE FORCES AT WORK

1 Social, cultural and commercial forces

The world changes faster, yet more subtly and stealthily, than most people imagine. As with any ageing process, it is only when looking back that the pace and scope of the change are recognised, and even then the view is rarely complete. When assessing social and behavioural change and its consequences, new attitudes may appear only when prodded by a new business development, a major technological innovation or a social or political event. How social and cultural forces develop, where we are now and where we might be heading, are crucial to understanding how business strategy will need to evolve. Business operates in a wide economic, political and social context, and it is often said that the only constant is an ever-increasing rate of change. Yet what is driving that change, and what are the consequences for business strategy? Interestingly, the forces shaping business derive their strength and energy from these potent sources of social change.

One consequence of this is that a number of pillars of business orthodoxy are being eroded. Many attitudes and beliefs that were relevant thirty, ten or even only five years ago, are now less significant or of no consequence. If business decisions are to be effective, workable and sound, they must be grounded in the present and the likely future.

This chapter reviews the social, cultural and commercial influences that continue to change the world of business: how attitudes, behaviours and expectations are changing; what people expect as customers, employees and members of society, and the implications of this for business.

The changing world

The new economy may or may not materialise, but there is no doubt that the next society will be with us shortly. In the developed world, and probably in the emerging countries as well, this new society will be a good deal more important than the new economy (if any). It will be quite different from the society of the late 20th century, and also different from what most people expect. Much of it will be unprecedented. And most of it is already here, or is rapidly emerging.

Peter Drucker, *The Economist*, November 3rd 2001

Peter Drucker, a respected management guru, believes that the business world we know is changing structurally and, in all probability, forever.

Identifying what these changes are, what is driving them and what their effects will be is critical for the strategist.

Paradoxically significant

The modern world involves an increasing number of apparent contradictions. In business, it has become more and more important for organisations to be both local (or regional) and global, to be centralised in some ways and decentralised in others, to rely on people to be innovative and use their own expertise, but also to collaborate as part of a team, to plan for the long term yet remain responsive and flexible. In addition, business relies on "hard" management factors such as finance, technology and processes, yet also on "soft" factors such as leadership, communication and creativity. In the words of Charles Handy, a British management thinker and writer: "Everywhere we look, paradox seems to be the companion of economic progress."[1]

The reasons for this are not difficult to perceive. Competitive pressures, both for individuals and organisations, are driving this need to excel in new ways. Our ambition leads us to believe, correctly in most instances, that we can benefit from doing things in ways that seem contradictory to the ways things have traditionally been done. If we are adventurous yet disciplined, the result may be extraordinary and possibly unique in creating value and competitive advantage.

People and organisations now recognise that paradoxes can be reconciled, and they are more enabled to reconcile them than ever before, partly because of technological progress. For example, in the 1950s and 1960s, marketing was concerned with mass coverage, and issues such as share of voice and column inches were important; if more people heard about the product, then sales would increase. Computerisation during the 1970s and 1980s led to database marketing and customer profiling. In theory, only those customers likely to buy were targeted with marketing activity, reducing costs and increasing marketing efficiency. Holding data on individual customers became the new source of competitive advantage, and this led to new data-protection legislation from the mid-1980s. Then, in the 1990s, the internet and world wide web arrived on a mass scale, allowing the largely contradictory goals of mass marketing and niche targeting to be combined. The internet can reach millions of potential customers, but it is also possible, in theory at least, to relate individually to every single customer. The classic pioneers of this approach are the online bookseller or travel agent: with the mass appeal of a major retailer, they can also offer a personalised service. This new era of mass customisation has therefore overcome many contradictory difficulties.

This increasing rate of change, so far as leadership and decision-making are concerned, is highlighted by three great paradoxes:

- In an uncertain and fast-changing world, leaders must provide stability, certainty and a sound foundation. They must set out and communicate a consistent set of values and principles to make the process of change sustainable. In short, leaders must ground themselves in the certainty of a specific perspective, before leading people into a shifting, uncertain world of possibilities.
- Leaders need information to understand the complexities of their environment and to ensure effective action. Yet the amount of information available these days is overwhelming, with the potential for "paralysis by analysis". Again, traditional leadership values are important, and the solution is often to work through a consistent set of principles that enables you to capture and filter relevant knowledge, and then transform this into effective action.
- Leaders need to be both proactive and reactive, managing planned and emerging issues with equal success. This juggling act is difficult. Too often, businesses are either wedded to strategies and plans, focusing on a long view that may be undermined by events, or they are fire-fighting, reacting to circumstances, with little or no prospect of achieving steady and sustainable growth.

Getting the balance right between seemingly conflicting issues is what counts. The secret to understanding and managing apparent paradoxes is in the timing. Contradiction emerges only when a situation is viewed over time, because at any one moment, one factor or the other is in the ascendant. It is like a seesaw: over time, both sides are in the air and both are on the ground, but at any one moment only one side is up and the other is down. Similarly, with a team, some tasks are done together and others are completed individually. None of this is new. The difference is the increase in the number of apparent conflicts and their heightened significance, the fact that complexity, contradiction and paradox can be used to powerful effect.

All change – as things do

Three important and closely related developments affecting the way that people are employed have gathered pace over the past decade. First, organisations increasingly outsource activities relating to managing people. Second, organisations rely more on people that are neither full-time nor permanent employees. Third, and most significantly, people are increasingly seen not just as employees but also as valuable assets. Consequently, employees are changing their attitudes to work, and the nature of loyalty and duty in society is changing. The impact on strategic decisions requires an understanding of the forces driving these trends and an acceptance of the responsibilities and priorities that emerge.

The past 50 years have brought greater education, greater freedom of expression and thought, more equality, the erosion of traditional hierarchies and deference, greater social and geographic mobility of labour and many other social changes. A century ago, millions of people worked in large and intimidating factories, accepting a hierarchical and paternalistic management structure. They later formed unions to protect their rights and their livelihood. Meanwhile managers directed and controlled on a mass scale, and the art and science of management took shape. When commanded to fight and, if necessary, die during the two world wars, they did. Today, unions are weaker, factories employ considerably fewer people, those that are employed are more skilled and educated, hierarchies are flatter and loyalties to employers are less strong. It is difficult to imagine millions of conscripted people in the developed world marching to war as they did twice in the 20th century – and not just because the nature of warfare has changed. In the workplace, social change has necessitated an ability to manage change, show leadership, build teams, be innovative, manage knowledge and allow flexible working in order to benefit both organisations and those who work for them.

Societies change

More women are employed than ever before, and many want flexible careers. They are not alone: men also want greater flexibility. Demographic trends in developed countries indicate that populations are ageing; increasingly some people choose to work past traditional retirement ages, often part-time.

Looking beyond the developed world, companies are adopting different views of developing countries. During the latter half of the 20th century, the prevailing business logic was that, as their economies expanded, countries such as India, China, Brazil, Bulgaria and others in

Asia, Latin America and central Europe were ready sources of cheap labour and potentially profitable new markets. However, globalisation has made companies aware that in these countries there are pools of talented and capable people, so they are increasingly keen to employ Indian or Bulgarian software designers, not only because they are less expensive, but also because they are often better and more reliable. Businesses are beginning to understand the potential for skilled labour in parts of the world that they had previously ignored.

People change

People are accepting that there are no longer "jobs for life", and many would not want to stay in the same job throughout their working life. Individuals are likely to have several, even many, employers during their career. They are also changing their attitudes to work. Studies by the Commission of the European Union and the United States Department of Labour have highlighted that people work longer average hours than they used to, and are often prepared to work flexible hours. In return, they expect greater job satisfaction, higher rewards, more personal recognition and a more flexible work environment.

Changing patterns of employment: Ricardo Semler and Semco

Ricardo Semler, a Brazilian businessman, is a maverick, a prophet of the new, changing patterns of employment. His company, Semco, was transformed from a struggling machine business into a profitable, innovative and exciting corporation in a few years, through the aggressive application of employment policies and procedures that recognised how work patterns were changing.

Semler holds the widely accepted view that people are valuable and unique: they can participate in local and national democracy, contribute to the community, raise children, express themselves through hobbies and other activities and have the knowledge and potential of the internet at their fingertips. However, when they go to work they are treated, en masse, as robots. He therefore set about finding ways to recognise, respect, reward and liberate his workers. For him, the answer was not simply to graft empowerment on to an existing hierarchical structure. He took a more radical approach, with workers empowered (if they wished) to find out about, discuss and help set the direction of the business and implement it. For example, employees were able to decide what their targets and salary levels should be, as well as other issues traditionally left to senior managers. This approach allowed talent throughout the organisation to flourish. Furthermore, employees were paid not according to hierarchy or status, but according to the real value, meaning the scarcity, of what they did. This may seem like a socialist Utopia, but it actually gave Semco's employees great individual responsibility, which they accepted. Individuals were given a much greater say in how their business fared and much greater control of their fate.

Semler recognises the difficulties inherent in this approach:

> At first it was hard for us. But with a great deal of commiseration and consultation the shock of the rulelessness began to subside, and our middle managers began to remove their armour plates. I like to tell them that a turtle may live for hundreds of years because it is well protected by its shell, but it only moves forward when it sticks out its head.[2]

Interestingly, Semler's views of changing employment patterns extend to his personal life. He sets his priorities for the day and then works to achieve them. When they are accomplished, he can go home to spend time with his family. Depending on events and how the work progresses, he may finish at lunchtime or midnight, but what he does not do is set an interminable list of tasks to accomplish. If managers do this, he believes, they are simply putting undue pressure on themselves, resulting in demotivation, impaired judgment and reduced performance.

Organisations change

Competitive pressures for greater flexibility, productivity and cost control are driving changes in the way that organisations are employing people, and social and demographic changes are affecting what people want and expect from work. Whereas traditional philosophers such as Karl Marx believed in a fundamental schism between the needs of the employer and those of the worker, in truth, their interests are in many ways symbiotic, each needing and valuing the other.

Increasing flexibility requires people to have a variety of skills that relate not only to the tasks they can accomplish but also the levels at which they work. And they must be willing to develop existing skills and learn new ones. Similarly, management structures must be able to adapt – respond and learn, focus and co-ordinate. Organisations with unnecessary, misunderstood bureaucracy that hampers this flexibility must change or risk decline. The pressing goal is to focus on adaptive organisational learning, where sensing and understanding changes in the external environment is routine, and the ability to respond swiftly and effectively is ever-present. Employees must be trained in the skills they will need. Reward systems should encourage people to take up and apply new skills.

To be more productive, organisations require the right people and the right resources in position at the right time. They must also instil a culture that encourages continuous learning and improvement. This places important, and new, obligations on decision-makers. Among the many factors that help drive productivity, measurement techniques have increasingly been seen as important, hence the popularity since the 1990s of benchmarking, the balanced scorecard and key performance indicators (KPIS). David Norton, co-author with Robert Kaplan of *The Balanced Scorecard*,[3] believes that "you cannot manage what you cannot measure". Donald Marchand, co-author of *Making the Invisible Visible*,[4] takes this view further: "You cannot manage what you cannot measure, and you cannot measure what you cannot see." Marchand's research conducted at IMD, a business school in Lausanne, Switzerland, has identified a link between investments in people, information and technology and bottom-line performance. This emphasis on measurement is being embraced by a diverse range of organisations worldwide.

Employers change
The need to find new ways to compete has led organisations to focus on reducing both the costs and risks of employing people. This explains the rise of professional employee organisations (PEOS), which supply highly skilled temporary workers. Companies increasingly appreciate the benefits of employing people on fixed-term, temporary or part-time contracts. Employment costs are reduced, and the legal liabilities can often be effectively "outsourced" to PEOS. Many statistics highlight the increasing role of PEOS and the benefits they can provide:

- The annual cost of government regulations and tax compliance for US businesses employing fewer than 500 people was estimated at approximately $5,000 per employee.[5] Using temporary workers can eliminate these as well as the direct costs of employing someone.
- The risk associated with employment can sometimes be managed more effectively using PEOS. For some this is a contentious and even worrying development. However, between 1980 and 2000 the number of general US regulations regarding employment practices grew from 38 to 60, and the fines for non-compliance, even if unintentional, can be severe.

■ Worldwide, as many as 10m temporary workers are placed each day. These are not just the traditional receptionists and secretaries, but virtually every type of office worker.

Between 1991 and 2000, the number of sexual harassment cases filed annually in the United States soared from 6,900 to nearly 16,000. Avoiding many of these claims is seen as one of the advantages of PEOS. Furthermore, for every case filed, ten are estimated to settle out of court. It is not surprising, therefore, that in the United States there are 1,800 PEOS. By 2005 it is estimated that they will employ an estimated 10m workers.[6]

Providing effective leadership for all of the people contributing to the productivity and performance of the organisation is clearly harder to achieve in what Drucker calls "the splintered organisation". Employment policies assume that most people working for an organisation are employees, whereas increasingly they are not (though see below with regard to employee rights). This matters because the foremost challenge amid change and splintering is to oversee effectively: ensuring that the many different types of people working for an organisation are pulling in the same direction and that their efforts are co-ordinated. Legislative changes to take account of this change in employment patterns are being considered; for example, the European Union is planning to give temporary workers similar rights to full-time workers, but how far this protection may extend, and when, is far from certain.

Outsourcing has delivered many benefits, aiding flexibility, efficiency and competitiveness. At the same time outsourcing is not an easy option; it requires careful management. There are many examples of projects, including several major IT projects in Britain's public sector, that have been outsourced and failed to deliver as intended. Nevertheless, strategic decisions must take account of changing patterns of employment as well as the talents, values and aspirations of an organisation's workers.

Knowledge matters
It has become evident that what will matter in the future are an organisation's collective skills and knowledge and how they are managed. This is not to say that knowledge workers providing scarce or unique sources of insight will outnumber other types of employees, but rather that the success, and even the survival, of organisations will come to rely increasingly on the performance of its knowledge workers. Thomas

Stewart, author of *Intellectual Capital* and a prominent writer in this field, has commented that:

> *Knowledge has become the most important factor in economic life. It is the chief ingredient of what we buy and sell, the raw material with which we work. Intellectual capital – not natural resources, machinery or even financial capital – has become the one indispensable asset of corporations.[7]*

So what exactly is meant by the term knowledge worker? Drucker first introduced the term in his 1969 book *The Age of Discontinuity*.[8] Recognising that the "corporate man" would not last forever, Drucker perceived the ascendancy of the highly trained, intelligent managerial professional, who understands his own worth and contribution to the organisation. Knowledge work is highly specialised and can therefore splinter organisations. Consider the range and depth of skills and knowledge needed to manage a chain of retail stores, a hospital, a university, an automotive manufacturer or a financial services business. As the scope and complexity of what we can achieve and what our customers expect deepen, the challenge to keep this expertise co-ordinated and moving in the right direction becomes greater. The task of employing knowledge in order to achieve this is crucial.

Knowledge is both ownership (by the knowledge worker) and power, a decisive source of competitive advantage. In the words of Lew Platt, former CEO of Hewlett-Packard, "If H-P knew what it knows, we would be three times as profitable." Driven by the ability to find, retain and analyse information, resulting from the worldwide growth of technology and the internet, new and decisive sources of competitive advantage have emerged.

Flowing from this is the concept of intellectual capital, an asset that is created from knowledge. As Stewart points out:

> *Intelligence becomes an asset when some useful order is created out of free-flowing brainpower ... organisational intellect becomes intellectual capital only when it can be deployed to do something that could not be done if it remained scattered round like so many coins in the gutter.*

The challenge is to make decisions that will use knowledge, turning it into intellectual capital.

Developing intellectual capital: Leif Edvinsson and Skandia[9]

One of the first people to quantify and value intellectual capital was Leif Edvinsson. Appointed in 1991 as the world's first director of intellectual capital at Skandia, Sweden's largest financial services corporation, Edvinsson views intellectual capital as being of three types:

- **human capital**, that which is in the heads of employees;
- **structural capital**, that which remains in the organisation; and
- **customer capital**, that deriving from the relationships the company enjoys with its customers. Customer capital is often seen as a subset of structural capital.

The aim of Skandia's measures is to track whether intellectual capital is increasing or decreasing, focusing the organisation's culture and thinking on increasing its intangible assets. In Edvinsson's view:

> Intellectual capital is a combination of human capital – the brains, skills, insights and potential of those in an organisation – and structural capital – things like the processes wrapped up in customers, processes, databases, brands and systems. It is the ability to transform knowledge and intangible assets into wealth-creating resources, by multiplying human capital with structural capital. This is the intellectual capital multiplier effect.

At Skandia, human capital is further divided into several elements: customer focus, process focus and renewal and development focus. Edvinsson has designed a process for each business unit to report on all of these areas of intellectual capital. The importance placed on his work was highlighted by the inclusion in Skandia's annual report of the value of its intangible intellectual capital assets, which was estimated at more than $15 billion. However, for Edvinsson the real benefit has been even greater: managing intellectual capital has nurtured innovation and new thinking and has helped create a mindset that will enable Skandia to compete more effectively in the future.

The rise of knowledge and intellectual capital suggests that to be successful, organisations will need to focus on:

- the reconfiguration of existing systems (including the organisational culture) to support knowledge workers;
- the creation of a learning organisation that is constantly sensing, valuing and sharing information and using it in a flexible way to improve efficiency, generate profitable new ideas and, overall, add value for customers;
- productivity improvements, through training and coaching employees at all levels and through freeing managers to manage people.

Scarcity matters

The theory of supply and demand lies at the heart of market economics. Profitability requires scarcity, and this is increasingly provided by the uniqueness of knowledge. The more abundant the supply of a good or service, the lower its price will be, even to the extent that it may not be profitable to produce and sell. The more scarce the supply, and when competition is held back by barriers such as patents, expertise or other forms of knowledge, the more likely the good or service is to generate a profit. Where there are such barriers, the price of a good or service no longer relates directly to its cost of production but rather to its customer value, which in turn relates to its uniqueness or the costs that buyers would incur if the product were not available. In the pharmaceuticals industry, if there is a high demand for a product for which you have a patent and no alternative exists, the future is a lucrative one, even if the R&D costs have been substantial. Thus scarce and valuable knowledge can help deliver exceptional profits.

Organisations should therefore focus on opportunities where they may benefit from scarcity, keeping a special eye on the future. Where does scarcity lie and where is it likely to develop? In our finite world, there will always be bottlenecks, blockages or things that there is a need for but which are unavailable. But because someone somewhere will come up with innovative solutions, the scarcity will not remain the same for long. Having the insight and knowledge to understand such changes is as important as the ability to then deliver customer value. And if you can anticipate the changes, you will be ahead of the competition.

Thus to make effective strategic business decisions, it is essential first to develop an understanding of how, why and where scarcity will occur, and then to use people's skills and abilities to deliver new sources of customer value that are difficult to replicate and may be unique.

More demanding customers

Customer expectations have been encouraged to rise ever since the early 1980s, when *In Search of Excellence* by Tom Peters and Robert Waterman[10] highlighted a need for greater focus on and consideration of the customer. The internet poses unusually difficult strategic challenges for businesses wanting to prosper from it. It has given customers a taste of fast, flexible, tailored, cost-effective solutions. It is often used to deliver customer value and meet customer needs in a highly competitive environment. Moreover, the better the service customers receive and the more they are courted, the more they will expect in the future.

The concept of value innovation, which builds on customer value, is fast gaining support. The argument is that what matters to customers (and so to businesses) is not simply the need to compete – the trap of competition – but rather the need to redefine the market in ways that generate powerful and distinctive new benefits for the customer. As an example, consider the case of Xerox and Canon, both competing for control of the copier market in the 1970s. In the early 1970s, Xerox held a 95% market share of the global copier industry. Its target customers were large corporations and its concept of customer value was that of centrally controlled photocopying. Xerox focused on manufacturing and leasing complex high-speed photocopiers to corporate copying centres, using its own manufacturing and sales service teams to provide a complete package. Then in the mid-1970s, Canon, a Japanese manufacturer and an industry newcomer, set about creating entirely new market segments for copiers not served by Xerox in the United States: small organisations and individuals. In the late 1970s, Canon designed a value delivery system offering a $1,000 personal copier to target these segments. For almost a decade, Xerox largely ignored this new business threat.

Canon focused first on overcoming the problem of patents, dedicating its research efforts to develop an alternative to Xerox's patented technology. The next line of attack was Canon's ability to redefine the customer base by designing personal copiers at a price point significantly below Xerox's big copiers, appealing to small businesses and individuals. The price range of Canon's personal copiers was $700–1,200, whereas that of Xerox's high-speed large-volume machines was $80,000–129,000. However, the specification offered by Canon was all that many businesses and individuals required. Next, Canon reviewed the issue of distribution. It rejected the direct salesforce approach favoured by Xerox, choosing instead to distribute its personal copiers through third-party distributors such as office-supply firms, computer stores and retailers. This did not require a huge cash outlay. It also allowed rapid market entry.

Xerox's inability to maintain a dominant or even a significant position in the photocopying industry resulted in a rapid slide down the *Fortune* 500. Three decades on, it is even more crucial to be alert to customer needs that are not being satisfied.

However, while it is clear that many business gurus have encouraged the view that delighting the customer is everything, it appears that, despite years of tender loving care, many customers do not feel delighted or well served. Many customers take innovations and service as routine. Stephen Brown, a professor of marketing research at the University of Ulster in Northern Ireland, argues that customers often enjoy being tantalised and teased, and are frequently repelled by strangers trying too hard to be their "best friend". The development of the internet has brought with it many stories of organisations that have so much information about customer preferences and such a ham-fisted way of using it that they drive their customers away rather than retaining them.

The idea that innovation itself should be customer-driven is also being challenged and re-examined. If customer-driven simply means delivering real, appreciated and scarce value for customers, then it is welcome. However, if it means that customers, who often do not know quite what they want or are not expert enough to know what is possible, are required to do the thinking and driving (perhaps in focus groups), then the tail is wagging the dog. Customers are rarely a homogeneous group, so it is crucial to decide which customer group is being targeted. In the end, however, when the desires of the target market have been ascertained, the task of delivering what is desired rests with the organisation.

Globalisation's big effect

Globalisation brings both opportunities and challenges; it liberates and constrains; it creates the largest markets ever known and allows the potential players to be smaller than ever. If the future business world has a greater number of paradoxes, then globalisation will spawn many of them. What are the forces arising from globalisation that affect strategy?

First, power is increasingly out of proportion to size. What matters in the global economy is not simply size; it is other intangible factors such as scarcity or reputation. Organisations that have something scarce and valuable are now able to exert a massive amount of power and influence. Previously that scarcity was competed for only within a local or national market; now the potential demand is much bigger. So either the price rises or the volumes increase: whatever happens the business benefits. Microsoft is a prime example. A business established little over two decades ago now supports millions of enterprises and people with its software; its revenues and profits dwarf many nation states. It continues to do so not simply because it is now huge and has developed such a powerful position in the market, but largely because of its intellectual property and brand recognition and reputation. Whether Microsoft will continue to enjoy such success will depend largely on how effectively it identifies customer needs and how innovative it is.

Second, the developments behind globalisation, notably in technology, require that organisations act swiftly and flexibly if they are to stay ahead of the competition. People have been able to travel the world for the past 500 years; the difference now is that they are connected immediately. The internet boom of the 1990s made people realise that business could operate, more or less unconstrained by geography, 24 hours a day, 7 days a week and 365 days a year. This new, faster-moving, faster-changing business environment has driven companies of all sizes to organise themselves into smaller, more responsive, focused units. Affected by increasing competition in their global market, logistics firms such as DHL and FedEx have responded by enabling their customers to track their packages as they are transported. For large companies whose sheer size makes them more difficult to manage, it can be hard to make themselves as flexible and responsive as smaller units are able to be. As Jack Welch, former CEO of General Electric, said:

> What we're trying relentlessly to do is to get that small company soul – and small company speed – inside our big company body.

Third, the more global we become, the more tribal is our behaviour. John Naisbitt, author of *Global Paradox*, argues that the more we become economically interdependent, the more we hold on to what constitutes our core basic identity.[11] Fearing globalisation and, by implication, a homogenised western (predominantly American) culture, such countries as Indonesia, Russia and France have passed laws to preserve their distinctiveness and identity. Matters are further complicated by the shift from traditional nation states to networks. The role of diasporas in developing the economic and political fortunes of many countries is significant, as is seen in the role of the Chinese diaspora in driving the economic development of many Asian states. According to *The Economist*:

> *Emigrés of one kind or another send about $100 billion home each year through official channels, 60% of it to poor countries, which may receive another $15 billion unofficially.*[12]

This change may be neither uniform nor as powerful as some believe. Mankind is gregarious; valuing community and the ability to share information and form allegiances across borders can reduce tribalism. But cultural issues run deep and must be taken into account in strategic decisions. The merger of Daimler, a German automotive firm, and US-based Chrysler highlighted huge cross-cultural problems of organisational and management culture, and, by all accounts, there was much tribalism to contend with as well.

Fourth, globalisation has also led to the realisation that there are many geographic opportunities beyond the current sphere of operations. Keith Whitson, CEO of HSBC, a multinational financial services firm, commented in August 2002 that the performance of call-centre employees in China and India was far superior to that of their British counterparts:

> *Staff are hugely enthusiastic about their jobs. In all cases the performance in the UK is inferior.*

In the past, poor countries remained poor and rich countries remained rich for generations. If a country's fortunes changed, then typically it occurred over many generations. Now societies develop skills, wealth and commercial opportunity in a much shorter time. In the early 1960s, South Korea's GDP was on a par with that of present-day Sudan. In 1945, Japan and Germany were physically destroyed and largely friendless in the arena of international trade and long-term development. Within a generation, they had become the second and third richest countries in the world. Although the economic performance of both countries currently lags behind others, they remain the second and third largest economies, with among the best standards of living. Conversely, at the start of the 20th century Argentina was a leading economic power; now it is in economic disarray. The point is that international sources of strength and capability change. When considering where economic growth might be assured in the future, the

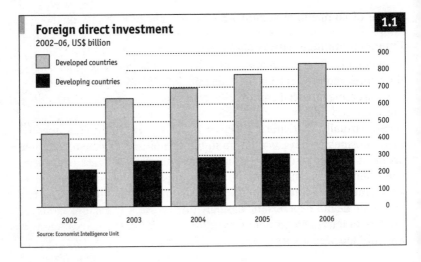

Foreign direct investment
2002–06, US$ billion

- Developed countries
- Developing countries

Source: Economist Intelligence Unit

ten countries invited to join the European Union in 2004 (Lithuania, Estonia, Latvia, Czech Republic, Hungary, Slovakia, Slovenia, Poland, Cyprus and Malta) seem sensible prospects.

It is certainly true that global foreign direct investment (FDI), a significant measure of globalisation, having risen from $160 billion in 1991 to $1.5 trillion in 2000, has since shrunk back to about $650 billion in 2002.[13] However, this is much more to do with a downturn in the developed economies and particularly a sharp drop in mergers and acquisitions.

It is in developing economies that globalisation continues to grow steadily, if slightly less spectacularly, with FDI expected to increase by 50% during the period 2002–06 (see Figure 1.1). This growth is driven by a growing appreciation in the West of the opportunities these markets can provide, combined with a growing understanding of how best to do business in developing markets.

One region that should continue to develop economically is Asia. Japan, South Korea, Hong Kong, Singapore and Taiwan started the process, and Thailand, Malaysia and Vietnam have all grown rapidly in recent years. But the biggest powers of all, India and China, on top of the strides they have made, show massive, unfulfilled, economic potential. Eastern Europe (notably Poland) and Latin America (Mexico in particular) are other regions possessing significant economic potential. When western markets falter, it is often developing economies that are seen as offering the greatest growth potential. The ability to find commercial opportunities in unlikely places is an increasing source of competitive advantage.

Financial management is changing

Traditionally, financial management has been largely about producing the figures required for business decisions to be made and establishing and enforcing financial controls. Recent years have seen a rise in the significance and influence of the chief financial officer (CFO) to the point where virtually no major decision is made without the CFO's involvement. Businesses have woken up to the complexities of financial management and the CFO now has major responsibilities in managing risk, controlling costs, increasing brand equity, maximising shareholder value, measuring financial performance and determining strategy. Thus corporate health depends increasingly on the finance function, as shareholders in Enron, Marconi and WorldCom and many other companies are only too well aware.

Rethinking the budget: Diageo[14]

Diageo was created following the 1997 merger between Guinness (a brewing conglomerate) and GrandMet (one of the world's largest producers of branded spirits), and its subsidiaries include Pillsbury and Burger King. Following the merger, 60 finance managers from all parts of the business met to discuss how they could best serve their shareholders in the future. Overwhelmingly, the response was to "blow up the budget". The feeling was that the budget process consumed vast resources, took too much time and took too little account of each individual business: there was a one-size-fits-all approach. There was little benefit for the shareholders in this detailed process (which is replicated in many corporations). The budgeting exercise was seen as a game, and the managers of the business understood that shareholders were concerned not about performance against arbitrarily agreed targets but about whether the company was worth more this year than last. As one senior finance manager commented:

> Everyone knew that something had to be done – we were wasting too much time and money. We began streamlining the current system's workload and progressed to creating an integrated strategic and annual planning process built around key performance indicators (KPIs) and rolling forecasts ... [We] focused on developing strategy-driven KPIs that were interconnected up and down the organisation. This ensured that people at every level and position had relevant metrics, while giving the

*board the right information to plan with. The same data, slightly
modified, enabled business units to operate most productively.*

Diageo went further than this, preferring externally oriented and forward-looking performance indicators to historical or internally focused ones. In this way, issues such as leading market indicators and brand equity become apparent. The result is a management focus that is concerned with resolving strategy issues and preparing for the future rather than dwelling on presentations of past figures and performance. The previously unsung and currently burgeoning talents of finance experts made this inevitable; they have much more to offer than simply tallying past events. Other business leaders, and in particular shareholders, want finance personnel to help them get the greatest value from every asset, including the expertise in their finance department.

Technology makes all the difference

In *Competing with Information*,[15] Donald Marchand and his co-authors highlight the breadth of the practical, commercial applications of technology. The most successful and effective organisations use technology for market sensing, innovation, flexibility, learning, selling, competing for and keeping customers, managing supply chains and improving efficiency, managing risk, motivating, leading and empowering. Much has been learnt about the role and application of technology, but more remains to be learnt about what it can do and, in particular, how to use it. As Marchand says:

*Information can be used to develop and sustain competitive
advantage, it is the way people in organisations express,
communicate and share their knowledge with others, to
accomplish their activities and achieve shared business
objectives. If knowledge – our experience, skills, expertise,
judgment and emotions – primarily resides with people, then
by using information, people can inform each other and be
informed about the decisions, actions and results of their work
in companies. It is through information about markets,
customers, competitors, partners, internal operations and the
mix of products and services offered by the organisation, that
managers and employees create business value and improve
performance.*

In *Making the Invisible Visible*,[16] Marchand highlights a critical and decisive factor: the way that people and technology interact. Companies spend huge sums on their technology systems, with little direct understanding of how that investment directly affects profits. How technology enhances business strategies and decisions is covered in Chapter 13, but it is helpful to understand the following:

- Managers will increasingly need to develop an integrative view of the way that people, information and IT work together. IT specialists are, of course, important in supporting an organisation's effective use of information, but it is others who need to understand how to integrate processes, structures, behaviours and values in order to set the strategic route and follow through.
- Organisations must discern where and when technology can be deployed to facilitate the effective use of information. Senior managers, who are not IT specialists, should decide which IT investments and applications are appropriate and when IT investments will not necessarily lead to improvements in information management or produce better results. Business leaders must develop the ability to balance the opportunities, risks and investments in technology with their people's ability to use information to add value and improve performance.
- Organisations must create the conditions for effective information use. Information management is the responsibility of every manager and information responsibility, as Drucker[17] calls it, means that managers have to discover what information they need, how that information should be provided, and who will supply it and when.

Also important is how well the organisation uses information to create value. According to Marchand:

> *Information management responsibilities exist at the level of the individual manager and business unit at the same time. Managers must understand how they use information with those around them and how their company creates business value with information.*

Senior management must, therefore, ensure that information use is as intelligent, co-operative and focused as possible on the goals of the organisation. Those who are in the know have huge power, so it is in everyone's interests that managers should be fully aware of how they use information to make decisions. If they are not, they will find their competitive advantage dwindling.

Demographic challenges

Demographic changes are likely to have a dramatic effect over the next 20–50 years. Significant reductions in the number of people in both the developed and developing world will affect the availability of skills, the size and dynamics of markets, and the value of many key resources. Such changes will have a big impact on businesses and the decisions they make.

The world's population is likely to fall. For the population to stand still, each woman needs to have 2.1 children (one child per parent, plus an extra 0.1 to account for women who die young, are infertile, or otherwise do not have children). This is known as the replacement level. Today more than 60 countries, including China, Germany, Greece, Japan, Korea, Russia, Spain and the United States, as well as much of eastern Europe and the Caribbean, have fertility rates below this level, and the trend is deepening and extending to other countries. The UK's replacement rate is 1.7 and Italy's is 1.2. Within the next 20 years the fertility rates of Brazil, India, Indonesia, Iran, Mexico, Sri Lanka, Thailand and Turkey will fall below the replacement level.

At this rate, Italy's current population of 56m would crash to 8m by 2100; Germany's would decline by 85% over the same period from 80m to 12m; and Spain's would decline by 83% from 39m to 6.6m. However, just as fears of increasing population rates resulted in forecasts of disaster during the early 1970s, highlighted by the Club of Rome's *Limits to Growth* report, tales of populations falling by over three-quarters are probably exaggerated, not least because they will be alleviated by the effects of immigration. Nonetheless, populations are likely to fall. As the *New Scientist* reported: "Within two generations four out of five of the world's women will be having two children or fewer."[18]

So what are the likely consequences for businesses?

- More women will work at all levels in organisations, and will increasingly compete with men for higher-status jobs. Women's emancipation and moves to more equal status have driven a string of changes reflecting women's priorities and increased purchasing power.

■ The technological development that transformed the 20th century will continue. With fewer traditional workers, even in the developing world, and an increasing need to industrialise poorer countries, technology will be used to raise productivity globally.

■ Some markets and industries will contract and others will expand. This will potentially have an impact on many sectors, from healthcare to agriculture.

When populations change, social change follows. For example, when there is a decreasing number of working people to fund pensions, retirement ages may need to change, and immigration may need to be encouraged to ensure that there are people to do the jobs that need to be done.

What is driving change? An economist's view of technology

As well as changing the way in which organisations deliver value, technology is driving change in many other areas, affecting the context of strategic decisions. Laura D'Andrea Tyson, dean of London Business School and a leading economic adviser to Bill Clinton from 1996 until 2000, highlights the main force driving global change:

> The basic factor driving change is technology. It's trite to say but it's true. The two major developments taking place in the world are demographics and interconnectedness. Interconnectedness is about transportation and communication, and that's driven by technology. Demographics is actually about biotechnology and science.

She adds that demographics examines the causes of improved longevity. Technological advances have increased longevity and reduced disability. The impact of this change is felt in a number of areas, including retirement. Should people retire at 65 if they are going to live to 100? In advanced industrial societies, less time is spent in the workplace than on other activities because longevity has increased but working hours have not. People are staying at school longer and are retiring earlier.

The key to the future is how to make work-life more meaningful – now it's like a cliff, and when you retire you fall off that cliff ... There need to be alternatives or bridging mechanisms in place, to help people prepare for retirement. Technology is driving all of this.

Controlling businesses

A wave of financial and accounting scandals in the early years of the new millennium, involving, among others, Enron, WorldCom and Andersen, focused attention on the way that organisations are controlled. The possibility that even respected firms might be guilty of accounting shenanigans depressed stockmarket prices. How are we to regain faith in standards of corporate governance, and what are the implications for businesses?

The regulatory route

Supranational bodies, such as the European Union, have steadily increased regulations in areas such as corporate governance, data protection and employment. In 2002 the United States introduced the Sarbanes-Oxley Act, requiring CEOs to formally vouch for the accuracy of their firm's accounts. Developing countries, China being an important case, are recognising that an efficient capital market can only be achieved if there is intelligent and effective regulation of corporate activity and corrupt practices are weeded out. The intention is that this will redress the balance; however, as Lucy Kellaway, a journalist, comments:

> *Bureaucracy, after many years of decline, will be on the rise again. More regulation of companies, encouraged by the Sarbanes-Oxley Act in the United States, and other measures designed to clean up the corporate act will be the spur. The onus of proving that a company is whiter than white will bring huge time demands and a heavy paper trail with it.*[19]

Personality matters

Business history is full of the influence of people such as Henry Ford, Alfred Sloan, Akio Morita, Harold Geneen, Richard Branson, Jack Welch, Herb Kelleher and Bill Gates. But today charismatic business leaders are less able to influence the business environment. To some extent they can set the agenda, focus and direct, but they are much more vulnerable to internal and external factors. Charismatic leaders will always inspire but their organisations are likely to succeed only if there is a coherent, well-organised and imaginative team supporting them.

Key questions

- What is your organisation's most important asset (or greatest source of competitive advantage)? How secure is it?
- How well do your organisation's human-resources policies reflect changing patterns of employment? In particular, is your organisation co-ordinating the efforts and talents of all employees, enabling them to improve the organisation's effectiveness?
- Does the increasing flexibility of the labour market offer opportunities to improve organisational effectiveness, by reducing costs, increasing capability, or both?
- Is your organisation unnecessarily bureaucratic? Could it become more flexible, and if so, how?
- How can productivity be measured more effectively, and could these measures be enhanced? How can people in the organisation be encouraged to come up with ways in which productivity could be increased?
- Where does the intellectual capital of your organisation or business unit lie, and what can be done to develop and exploit it to gain long-term competitive advantage?
- How does your business involve customers? Are efforts made to understand what they want? Is the firm certain about what its customers value?

2 Ideas at work

Setting strategy is complex because of the complicated, shifting array of challenges and opportunities an organisation faces over time. For decision-makers to come to grips with this mounting complexity it helps to have an understanding of theories of management and leadership that have emerged during the past century.

Decision-making approaches
The classical administrator
The classical administrator is the most traditional model of the decision-maker or strategist. Henri Fayol is recognised as a founding father of this model, known as the classical school of management, which came into its own around 1910. He developed a set of common activities and principles of management, dividing general management activities into five sections: planning, organising, commanding, co-ordinating and controlling:

- Planning involves considering the future, deciding the aims of the organisation and developing a plan of action.
- Organising involves marshalling the resources necessary to achieve these aims and structuring the organisation to complete its activities. Both of these roles remain crucial.
- Commanding may be a term that is out of fashion in the egalitarian, politically correct and empowered world of many western organisations, but the concept remains significant. It is important to achieve the optimum return from people, frequently the most expensive component of a business.
- Co-ordinating involves focusing and, in particular, unifying people's efforts to ensure success.
- Control involves monitoring that everything works as planned, making adjustments where necessary and feeding this information back so that it can be of value in future.

The classical-administrator approach to decision-making is largely concerned with measuring and improving internal competencies in organisations. It is characterised by hierarchy, usually in the form of top-down planning and control, formal target setting and performance measurement, structured programmes for functional improvements through "scientific" engineering and a formal organisation structure. Fayol can be seen as a forerunner of modern management theorists who take a prescriptive view of strategic decision-making. For example, Frederick Taylor, one of the founding fathers of management theory in the first half of the 20th century, introduced a scientific-management approach to production department work; and Peter Drucker can be categorised as a classical administrator, at least in his approach to strategy development and decision-making.

The classical approach really took hold once entrepreneurs, such as Henry Ford, realised that they needed to focus on the productivity of their new manufacturing plants. It led to the development of efficient production lines and a focus on production quality, which started in the 1950s, built up efficiency in Japanese manufacturing industry and then took hold more widely in the 1980s. (This approach was publicised by W. Edwards Deming, an American who helped the Japanese improve their production processes in the early 1950s, although it was not until the early 1980s that his contribution to improving quality processes, and building a reputation for Japanese reliability, was recognised in his native land.) The emphasis on controlling and measuring foreshadowed the arrival of the total quality management movement. A *Fortune* magazine article in 1997 highlighted the significance of Taylor's work:

> It's his ideas that determine how many burgers McDonald's
> expects its flippers to flip or how many callers the phone
> company expects its operators to assist.[1]

Arguably this approach is for a different time and is no longer relevant. In Taylor's words:

> Nineteen out of twenty workmen throughout the civilised
> world firmly believe it is for their best interests to go slow
> instead of fast. They firmly believe that it is for their interest to
> give as little work in return for the money that they get as is
> practical.[2]

In this situation, a controlling, commanding and monitoring approach is probably vital, but even if this were once true, is it now?

The point is that it does not matter. The great value of the classical-administrator approach lies in the structured framework for action that it provides. Even in a time of quickening change, unknown variables and global complexity, a simple framework designed to organise and focus activities remains valuable for decision-making. (This process-driven approach provides the framework for rational decision-making and is outlined in Chapter 4.)

The design planner

The design-planning approach emerged in the mid-1960s, outlined by Alfred Chandler, Igor Ansoff and later by Kenneth Andrews. It empha-sises that the principal role of a leader is to plan the development of an organisation beyond the short term. This heralded the arrival of strate-gic thinking in organisations, as distinct from focusing on continuing management activities. In this approach, strategy results from a con-trolled and conscious thought process, achieving long-term competitive advantage and success, through answering questions such as: Where are we now? Where do we want to be? How are we going to get there?

This recognised, for the first time, that organisations are beset with turbulent change. In 1965 Ansoff wrote:

> *No business can consider itself immune to the threats of product obsolescence and saturation of demand ... In some industries, surveillance of the environment for threats and opportunities needs to be a continuous process.*[3]

Design planning requires expertise in two areas:

- ◢ anticipating the future environment, with the help of analytical techniques and models;
- ◢ devising appropriate strategies matching the external opportunities and threats to the organisation's resources, internal strengths and weaknesses.

Once the strategy is planned, it is simply a matter of using the tech-niques of the classical administrator to plan its implementation by, for example, having a master plan that schedules key tasks and budget-con-trolled activities.

The result was that strategic decision-making had been given a sepa-rate focus. Four decision types were identified, covering strategy, policy, programmes and standard operating procedures. The last three were already understood, with an emphasis on resolving recurring issues such as production efficiency. Actively shaping the future through decision-making was in the ascendancy. Ansoff classified decisions as:

- strategic, focusing on the dynamic issues of products and markets;
- administrative, concerned with structure and resource allocation; and
- operating, focusing on supervision and control.

These distinctions remain in the minds of decision-makers today, guiding their focus and actions.

The role player

Starting in the 1970s, Henry Mintzberg, a leading management thinker and writer, argued that the models of the classical and design theorists offered unrealistic views of how leaders and organisations work. Decision-making had been flawed and was incapable of understanding what actually happens in organisations, leaving them poorly placed to face the challenge of change. Mintzberg advocated the need to prescribe through description, to observe and assess the reality of strategy in action.

The role-player approach views the strategic decision-maker's job as more than that of a reflective and analysing planner and controller. What about the need for flexibility and swift responsiveness? What about the fundamental decisions that are made not at the top of the organisation, but much further down? For Mintzberg, vision, communication and negotiation, as well as the need to be able to react quickly to disturbances and to change tactics at short notice, are of greatest importance. Moreover, an ad hoc approach balances short-term needs with a longer-term understanding of environmental developments. Such an approach can emphasise the benefit of learning-by-doing decision processes, where strategies emerge in the context of human interactions, rather than resulting from deliberate and systematic planning systems. This is similar to the approach adopted by scenario planners such as Kees van der Heijden, a professor at Strathclyde Graduate School of Business, who favours the concept of a strategic conversation. (This concept is outlined in Chapter 6.) The decision-maker's role becomes one of learning, supporting and positively enabling, rather than directing. The result may be incremental progress rather than a big bang, but it is no less real or valuable.

The competitive positioner

The competitive positioner understands the power of the external environment and focuses almost exclusively on the task of achieving competitive advantage. This approach takes as its underlying premise the belief that market power produces above-average profits in a marketplace where competition is the defining characteristic. The main theorist behind this approach is Michael Porter, professor of business administration at Harvard Business School. (Chapter 8 discusses the relevance of competitive issues for strategic decision-makers.) The competitive positioner's main tasks are to understand and decide where the organisation is competing, and then align it so that it is able to gain advantage over its competitors.

Competitive forces include customers and suppliers, substitute products (which are increasing in significance because of the flexibility and choice provided by the online marketplace), and present and potential competitors. Future competitors may not be those that we recognise today, and new competitors may well enter by changing the rules of competition. To compete successfully against all this, the positioner may need to do any combination of the following: erect barriers to entry into its market, attract price premiums for its products, reduce operating costs below those of its competitors.

Core competencies are viewed as the key to achieving competitive advantage. Advocates of this view include Gary Hamel and C.K. Prahalad, two leading management gurus.[4] This adds another layer of issues to be considered, and it requires building competitive competencies: those capabilities and sources of value that are scarce and cannot easily be replicated by competitors. Astute industry analysis also matters, to enable the development of winning competitive strategies and their successful implementation. Lastly, this approach emphasises the issue of market differentiation and the need to make decisions that build customer loyalty, as well as delivering higher quality and productivity.

The visionary transformer

Sounding like a fantastic new electrical appliance, the visionary transformer came to prominence in the 1980s, largely as a result of Tom Peters and Robert Waterman.[5] They saw vision as one of the fundamental tools of an effective strategic decision-maker, regarding issues such as:

- Where should the organisation position itself in the market to provide growth, to continue to build shareholder value and to keep ahead of its competitors?

- What type of organisation should it be? What are the brand values and aspirations of the organisation, and what do they need to be to realise its aims?
- What guiding principles steer the organisation, and how are they best assessed, communicated and applied? (This sense of mission is seen as essential; people that understand the core goals and values of the organisation are better placed to work towards these ends.)
- How should the organisation ensure that it is co-ordinated and working in concert? (This echoes Fayol's and Taylor's belief that co-ordination is a fundamental role of the classical administrator.)

Once these questions have been answered it is necessary to:

- develop and communicate a powerful, compelling vision of the future;
- structure and lead the organisation in the most effective and appropriate way;
- control the skills necessary to implement and realise the vision. These include energy and drive, dogged determination, a capacity for hard work, exceptional communication skills and the ability to empower and motivate others and to act as a role model.

However, visions must be achievable and visionary transformers must be capable of ensuring that they are achieved. An organisation that has an unrealistic view of its strengths and its market may find itself in trouble, as IBM did in the early 1980s, when it saw future profitability in the computer industry resting with hardware (largely ignoring software), and mistakenly thought that it could dominate the hardware market. Furthermore, it is not simply the vision that matters, but how that vision is developed and whether it is kept grounded in reality. Scenario planners can help an organisation keep in touch with reality both internally and with the external competitive environment.

The success of a visionary approach depends ultimately on pragmatism: the ability to achieve a vision through flexible, incremental and emergent activity through listening, acting and learning, rather than adopting plans or rigid approaches.

The self-organiser

In a complex and fast-moving business environment, there is an advantage to being a "learning organisation" that adapts to the winds of change. Peter Senge, author of *The Fifth Discipline*, highlighted this in 1993.[6] Self-organising businesses need to be designed and led by people who can create an organisation where its constituent parts and, above all, its people continually "self-organise" around emerging strategic issues, fluidly developing the organisation. In this way, accepted formulas and perspectives are constantly challenged and revised.

To achieve this, organisations need the ability to develop learning communities (networks of people working together without traditional top-down management to improve effectiveness) to generate innovative solutions for commercial opportunities. Innovation and collaboration are crucial competencies for operating in environments that are difficult to control and rapidly changing.

The turnaround strategist

This decision-making approach focuses on turning around the performance of an organisation in decline, perhaps when a visionary leader has failed. It is autocratic, ruthless and swift, and it is more context-specific. Invariably, the requirement is to operate when an organisation is in a state of crisis. Luc Vandevelde and Roger Holmes brought Marks & Spencer, a UK retailer that was for many years one of the UK's most admired companies, back from a decline that some thought might be terminal. Lou Gerstner turned around IBM after its dramatic decline by repositioning the business as a provider of services as well as a supplier of IT products. Turnaround strategy came into its own during the recession of the early 1990s, when many businesses feared for their survival.

To achieve turnaround success, it is important to implement new control systems quickly and to focus on the reasons for decline and reverse them, while going for the easiest route to immediate growth. Short-term issues are critical, and a dramatic change of overall perspective is required. Marks & Spencer and IBM also illustrate the importance of highlighting the causes of weakness, such as complacency, hubris and lack of vision, in order to change the culture and performance of the business.

The most effective approach

These different views of decision-making explain how new approaches to strategic leadership have developed. It is impossible to say that any one approach is more valid than another. Each approach gained support because of prevailing circumstances, and this is still the case. The most effective approach depends on the issues faced by an organisation, as well as the style and preferences of its leaders. Furthermore, each of these theories of management can be taken to reflect a particular leadership style, although, in reality, many organisations will reflect a mix.

Interestingly, these theories often build on earlier views, highlighting the debate among management theorists about how organisations can succeed in dynamic, challenging and often diverse environments. The development of a new approach means not that earlier ones should be discarded or are no longer valid, but that in certain circumstances they may no longer provide the best approach, at least on their own.

Clearly, in a complex world a mix of styles is needed, and the precise mix will depend on the personalities of those making the decisions. It is necessary to appreciate the strengths and weaknesses of your organisation, its environment and current position, and then to clarify, establish, sustain and acquire the competencies that are required, and to adopt the most appropriate leadership style to see the overall strategy realised.

It is likely that the underlying themes of the past century will remain significant for some time, and so understanding them is helpful. They include the following:

- The need for effective strategic leadership and decision-making at every level of an organisation.
- The need to forecast and manage uncertainty. This requires intuition, creative insight and the ability to respond to events quickly, effectively and imaginitively. It is not simply what we know that matters, but how we react to what we do not know. In a volatile, competitive and international commercial environment, organisations must be alert and adaptable. Continuous improvement is always to be valued, but there are times when more dramatic change is needed.
- The need to manage in adversity, such as a market collapse or the failure of a product. The organisation's structure and its culture and control systems must be flexible enough to enable swift decision-making and action to get matters back on course.

Financial issues

There can be few fields of human endeavour in which history counts for so little as in the world of finance.

J. K. Galbraith, *A History of Economics: The Past as the Present*, Penguin, 1987

The principal financial issues that influence strategic decisions are cash management, risk management and budgeting. As J.K. Galbraith, a highly respected economist, says, history is of little relevance here, though it can highlight the dangers of flawed decisions and the need for new approaches to be rigorous and combined with trusty (if dull) conventional methods. Financial management is essentially about managing future fortunes, and for this reason it dominates strategic decisions.

Cash management and cash flow

The link between financial management and strategy is pivotal. It is often said that without customers a business cannot exist. It is less often said, but no less true, that without finance (meaning the presence of cash rather than merely the prospect of it) a business cannot be sustained. Cash is the life-blood of any business and so it is invariably the biggest factor in strategic decisions: for example, whether to grow organically or by acquisition, how much to spend and when to spend it, and the payment terms to offer customers or seek from suppliers. When cash-management issues are not central to strategic decisions, the door to disaster is wide open.

Instant growth or bust: lessons from the dotcom collapse

The dotcom bubble was an example of what happens when sound, prudent and possibly boring attitudes to financial management are swept away in a wave of euphoria and hype. Decision-makers had overlooked a point made by Porter:

> Only by grounding strategy in sustained profitability will real economic value be generated. Economic value is created when customers are willing to pay a price for a product or service that exceeds the cost of producing it. When goals are defined in terms of volume or market share leadership, with profits assumed to follow, poor strategies often result.[7]

There were several financial truths that leaders of the new economy revolution failed to grasp:

◪ Investors' money was spent on technology and products because dotcom businesses thought they knew what customers wanted. In reality, they had no genuine understanding of customer needs or behaviour.

◪ Investment funds were often spent on driving market share, which in turn meant focusing on website visitors as opposed to paying customers. Phrases such as "first-mover advantage" and "winner takes all" were used to justify an approach that emphasised betting on tomorrow's success. Huge losses were racked up in the belief that it would all come good when the business took off, which, of course, few did.

They had ignored the economic fact that a business can only grow if it has real customers, not just virtual visitors. Sound, disciplined and prudent financial management would have exposed this uncomfortable truth and might have helped them succeed instead of fail.

Financial control

In recent years there have been some shocking examples of poor financial control. At Barings Bank, Sumitomo Bank and Allied Irish Bank, the activities of rogue traders were not picked up until huge damage had been caused. At WorldCom, Enron and Tyco, all kinds of malfeasance was occurring at a senior level resulting at the time in the largest bankruptcies the world had ever seen. Stewart Hamilton, a professor at IMD in Lausanne, Switzerland, and a commentator on issues of financial strategy and control, argues that:

> The key lessons for the financial sector of recent years are general management issues relating to the use of business information in managing risk – they are therefore highly relevant to all firms.[8]

Scandals often hit the headlines for a few days or weeks and are then forgotten, save for the publication of a dry, official report at some distant point in the future. The corporate scandals that hit the headlines in 2002 were, to some extent, an exception: they contributed significantly to upheavals on world stockmarkets and resulted in a raft of corporate changes, notably the Sarbanes-Oxley Act in the United States designed to clean up corporate affairs. Only time will tell whether the lesson that financial controls matter has been learnt, but the signs are that managers are at least aware of their importance.

___

When all is not lost, don't lose it: ensuring financial control

There has been much emphasis on the benefits of empowerment, on the fact that organisation structures are now flatter, more flexible and with much less stress on control than previously. As a result, the notion of control is out of fashion. However, there is one crucial area where empowerment and control need to work together effectively: financial management and decision-making. Without proper controls, financial management and in particular the management of risk remain uncertain, flawed activities. Control is necessary not only to avoid cheating or fraud, but also to test that the best decisions are made and that the most effective tactics are employed.

It is worth considering some examples of what can happen without effective control. The reputation of Morgan Grenfell Asset Management suffered when a fund manager was able to bypass the in-house rules and invest more than he was authorised to in unquoted equities.

> *Furthermore, he was able to set up a number of Luxembourg "front" companies to disguise his activities and continue to report excellent performance figures.*[9]

The affair embarrassed Deutsche Morgan Grenfell and was estimated to have cost the bank $700m, directly through compensation to investors and potential fines and indirectly through loss of clients.

___

Many of the biggest financial scandals occur in the financial services industry, but this is simply because that is where people have access to large sums of money. The problems of fraud or uncontrolled financial decisions by more junior staff are not limited to the financial sector. Every business needs adequate financials controls. This may seem to be stating the obvious, yet the reality is that in large corporations with flat management structures it is common for there to be inadequate controls at a practical level, at the point where decisions are made or expenditure incurred.

Controlling costs

Controlling costs is one way of boosting profits or reducing losses. During times of financial difficulty, everyone in an organisation should understand the need to save money, making cost-cutting a more achievable goal. During prosperous times cost control may seem less important, but the free-spending days of the dotcom boom made one thing clear: costs matter.

One of the most important factors in controlling costs is attitude. Fostering an understanding throughout an organisation of the financial facts of business life and the need to earn more than you spend makes a big difference. However, cost control issues vary according to the:

- type of industry, for example, whether it is a service or manufacturing business, or another sector such as governmental;
- type of business, for example, the issues a law firm may face will obviously differ from those faced by another service business, such as an advertising agency;
- maturity of the business, for example, a business start-up will take a different approach to cost control than a major multinational;
- culture of the business and the views and attitudes of its employees, suppliers, customers and shareholders;
- external environment and economic conditions.

Strategic decisions that actively control costs are explored in Chapter 12.

A new type of low-cost airline: Jean-Cyril Spinetta and Air France

One organisation that has pursued a successful strategy guided by a focus on cost control is Air France, under Jean-Cyril Spinetta, its chief executive. The airline business is volatile and has become tougher for mainstream airlines since 2001. However, Spinetta has presided over an airline widely regarded as efficient and well placed to weather storms that would have grounded other businesses. This can be attributed to several factors.

Understanding the business

Spinetta distinguishes between current crises affecting the business, such as cyclical downturns in the US economy or the events of September 11th 2001, and structural crises. Current crises are those that will affect the industry temporarily, and although they must be reacted to swiftly, the decisions they entail are different from those required for structural challenges. Following the terrorist attacks on New York and Washington in September 2001, initial expectations were that the crisis affecting the airline industry would last 12–18 months, yet after seven months passenger traffic at Air France was returning to normal.

Reducing costs and improving efficiency
The ability to distinguish between current and structural issues has helped turn around Air France's business since the 1980s and 1990s. Costs decreased between 1997 and 2002, but there have been unexpected additional costs: an extra US$100m annually for insurance, higher costs of security, higher operating fees payable to airports and air traffic control (to compensate for the overall reduction in air travel), and higher fuel prices. Spinetta launched a cost-reduction initiative in 1998, targeting reductions of €450m ($473m), and another three-year plan was launched in 2001, aiming to cut costs permanently by 5%. However, he is clear about what is involved:

> Even when things are going well, you have to be absolutely dedicated to decreasing costs. It is not something you have to do when things are difficult, it is something you have to do all the time and everywhere. Also, it is easier to reduce costs relatively and improve margins when you have a growth strategy, because you gain maximum efficiency from fixed costs [typically, more than 60% of airline costs are fixed]. So, the solution for Air France is to use capacity, improve cost control and efficiency, and innovate. The challenge is therefore in getting the most from those fixed costs to benefit customers. What matters is the efficiency of management strategy, alliances, motivating people, gaining market share in foreign markets.

To improve efficiency, Air France uses IT to capture customer information and as a measurement tool to improve the efficiency of sales and operations. IT is particularly valuable in helping to manage the logistics of a hub system, where passengers and their luggage need to be handled efficiently to ensure connections are made. Effective cost control is crucial to improving efficiency and growing the business. Spinetta believes:

> Achieving low costs is not so difficult. What matters is having the right costs and high motivation. If you have low costs and people are unhappy, then you have bad results. In the case of Air France, things have improved in terms of results, growth and reputation from the period 1982-96, and

people are reassured, proud and more positive. To achieve this we have a corporate plan that summarises the strategy of the company: communicating is essential, and people need to know Air France's priorities and vision. This is an important aspect of motivating people, and there is an ongoing process to develop, build and communicate the plan.

Setting realistic targets is also important. In the case of Air France, this led people to accuse Spinetta of lacking ambition, but over time they have come to understand, respect and be reassured by his approach. Targets for financial reserves were achieved, and this resulted in confidence. Clearly, it is better if the people running the business set the targets, rather than having them imposed by people who are not closely involved. Reliability in achieving the target matters as much as the target itself.

Long-term financial decisions and shareholder value

Shareholder value analysis (SVA) is a concept used for managing long-term financial decisions so that the value of the business is increased. SVA is founded on a view that standard accounting methods for calculating the value of a business are outmoded: either they dwell on a backward-looking historical perspective, or they are simply too short-term. Business decisions that are based on techniques such as price/earnings ratios or growth in profits are inadequate, because it is possible to make decisions which improve these measures in the short-term, such as reducing training or research expenditure, but which reduce the long-term value of the business.

The concept of shareholder value works from the premise that a business only adds value for its shareholders when equity returns exceed equity costs. SVA focuses on long-term profit flows, and so the analysis requires a long-term perspective, possibly involving significant change in what the organisation does and how it does it, as well as the business culture and skills of the workforce.

The principal features of SVA are as follows:

- It does not emphasise accounting measures for judging performance, preferring instead a more practical, context-sensitive approach that is better suited to individual businesses.
- It takes into account commercial risk and discounts future cash

41

flows (that is, it takes into account the time value of money) when making commercial, and particularly investment, decisions. With sva, financial considerations and techniques are much more to the fore when managers are making commercial decisions; issues such as return, risk, cash flow and value routinely guide managers in their operational as well as their strategic decisions.

◪ It requires more comprehensive commercial information across a range of factors, compared with traditional measures that only focus on a few short-term indicators, such as share price or quarterly profits.

See Chapter 11 for a more detailed guide to applying sva techniques.

The balanced scorecard approach

In their best-selling book *The Balanced Scorecard*,[10] Robert Kaplan and David Norton highlighted several ways in which business decision-makers can increase the long-term value of the business. Their approach applies the concept of sva and is based on the premise that the traditional measures used by managers to see how well their organisations are performing, such as business ratios, productivity, unit costs, growth and profitability, are only a part of the picture. These measures are seen as providing a narrowly focused snapshot of how an organisation performed in the past and giving little indication of likely future performance. In contrast, the balanced scorecard offers a measurement and management system that links strategic objectives to comprehensive performance indicators.

The success of this approach lies in its ability to unify and integrate a set of indicators that measure the performance of the activities and processes at the core of the organisation's operations. This is seen as being valuable because it presents a balanced picture of overall performance, highlighting activities that need to be completed. Furthermore, the balanced scorecard takes into account four essential areas of activity, of which the traditional "hard" financial measures are only one part. The three "soft", quantifiable operational measures include the following:

◪ Customer perspective: how an organisation is perceived by its customers.
◪ Internal perspective: those issues in which the organisation must excel.

Table 2.1 **Typical goals and measures**

Perspective	Goals	Measures
Financial	▰ Increased profitability ▰ Share price performance ▰ Increased return on assets	▰ Cash flows ▰ Cost reduction ▰ Gross margins ▰ Return on capital/equity/ investments/sales ▰ Revenue growth ▰ Payment terms
Customers	▰ New customer acquisition ▰ Customer retention ▰ Customer satisfaction ▰ Cross-sales volumes	▰ Market share ▰ Customer service and satisfaction ▰ Number of complaints ▰ Customer profitability ▰ Delivery times ▰ Units sold ▰ Number of customers
Internal processes	▰ Improved core competencies ▰ Improved critical technologies ▰ Streamlined processes ▰ Improved employee morale	▰ Efficiency improvements ▰ Improved lead times ▰ Reduced unit costs ▰ Reduced waste ▰ Improved sourcing/supplier delivery ▰ Greater employee morale and satisfaction and reduced staff turnover ▰ Internal audit standards ▰ Sales per employee
Innovation and learning perspective	▰ New product development ▰ Continuous improvement ▰ Employees' training and skills	▰ Number of new products ▰ Sales of new products ▰ Number of employees receiving training ▰ Outputs from employees' training ▰ Training hours per employee ▰ Number and scope of skills learned

◪ Innovation and learning perspective: those areas where an organisation must continue to improve and add value.

Managing for value: implementing the balanced scorecard

The type, size and structure of an organisation will determine the detail of the implementation process. However, the main stages involved include the following:

◪ Preparing and defining the strategy. The first requirement is to clearly define and communicate the strategy, ensuring that people have an understanding of the strategic objectives or goals and the three or four critical success factors that are fundamental to achieving each of these.

◪ Deciding what to measure. Goals and measures should be determined for each of the four perspectives: finance, customers, internal processes, and innovation and learning (see Table 2.1).

◪ Finalising and implementing the plan. Invariably, further discussions are necessary to agree the detail of the goals and activities to be measured and what measures should be used. Each measure needs an action to make it happen, and this is where the real value in the approach lies: deciding what action to take to achieve the goal.

◪ Once finalised, the plan needs to be communicated and implemented, with responsibility for different parts of the balanced scorecard being delegated throughout the organisation.

◪ Publicising and using the results. Although everyone should understand the overall objectives, it is also important to decide who should receive specific information, why and how often. Too much detail can lead to paralysis by analysis; too little and the benefits are lost, with too little action too late. The crux is to use the information to guide decisions, strengthening areas that need further action and using the process dynamically. Interestingly, evidence from businesses that have used this approach suggests that being seen to act can be as important as the action itself.

◪ Reviewing and revising the system. As with any management process, a final stage of review and revision is welcome, as this allows wrinkles to be smoothed out and new challenges to be set.

Essentially, the balanced-scorecard approach generates objectives in four business areas, and then involves developing action plans for them to be achieved, with progress being regularly assessed. One of the major criticisms of the approach is that it is overly prescriptive and scientific, being primarily concerned with measurement and quantitative rather than qualitative issues. But it does provide a structure, which can be adapted, for making decisions that are concerned with the long-term value of an organisation. It also allows for qualitative measures to be included and recognises that the four perspectives interrelate. As with any management tool or technique, the level of success achieved depends on the quality of the inputs and the way in which the system is implemented.

The rise and rise of technology

As the dotcom boom and bust showed, technology did not invent a new business paradigm, but it has transformed business, opening up a multitude of ways to add value, increase sales, reduce costs and manage more efficiently. Understanding the nature of this transformation is valuable for decision-makers.

The characteristics of internet-derived information

An information firestorm rages in most businesses, and how it is managed is crucial to success. A consequence of the increase in online activity is that information can be leveraged to create new sources of value. Yet it is important to combine the power of information and technology with common-sense approaches to management.

Online activity has, in a short period, dramatically increased the amount of commercial information available to businesses. Indeed, the ability to gather detailed and personalised customer information is helping to drive business growth, because of the potential benefits to customers and the opportunities for businesses. However, ensuring that the right information is available in the right place at the right time remains a challenge that few companies meet successfully. There is also the complex, frequently overlooked, yet crucial task of ensuring that traditional metrics and sources of information are enriched and not buried by the information explosion that so many organisations have experienced.

Learning by doing: using the internet to develop knowledge

An example of using information for development and innovation on the internet is the process of designing, releasing and improving software in the IT industry.

Software products like Microsoft Windows are rarely if ever developed with all the features and quality customers require. Instead, software is developed, launched and continuously improved. If the commercial proposition is right then customers will be pleased, and may prefer to go along with this approach, knowing that they will benefit from the continuous improvement process.

The standard product design, release and sell cycle applicable to cars, insurance, banking, consumer goods and industrial products does not apply to software. In the future, the standard cycle may apply less and less, as the internet provides:

- instant customer feedback on desired product features and enhancements;
- feedback on how effectively the desired features have been executed or delivered;
- the opportunity to sell once to customers a product that will be continually updated or enhanced, adding value for the customer and enhancing future cash flows for the business;
- the ability to take advantage of cost reductions to either reduce prices or enjoy increased margins.

There are other benefits, too, usually depending on the nature of the industry. Software features are continually tested in the market with groups of customers, and software products are released with known quality defects or bugs. This is because companies want to be early to market with their products, and they assume that bugs will be corrected with later versions. Software companies aim for modular releases of their products rather than grand designs, since customer acceptance of the product is always uncertain until it is used. Thus learning and doing in the software industry evolves continuously because of customer interactions and the responses of competitors.

Four characteristics of internet-derived information are critical to the discovery of new business opportunities and have an impact on decision-making:

1 **Information is digital.** All information on the internet must be in digital form. It can then be disseminated to a few or many at the click of a mouse. Finding out what customers need and how this can then be digitised and supplied is a potential opportunity. Several educational publishers, for example, realised that students, their end users, would value help with their homework assignments and therefore provided online

guides and tutorials, either selling bespoke services or repackaging traditional materials in online formats.

2 **Information is costly to produce, but cheap to reproduce.** Products should be priced according to what people will pay for them, rather than their cost of production. Furthermore, since reproducing information products is usually cheap, they can be made available to people and companies at very low marginal costs. This enables information-providing businesses to focus their spending less on delivery and more on other aspects of the business, such as selling and developing customer loyalty. However, the gathering of data about customers without a clear focus gives rise to the danger that customer data will simply overwhelm the business. A business must ensure information flows are actively managed, and only necessary, useful information is used.

3 **People must sample information to fully appreciate its value and benefit.** Information is what economists call an experience good. Often (but not always) customers do not know whether they will find an information product useful until they try it. With experience goods, the aim is to make the benefits widely known, with the aim of attracting people to try the product. An example of this is the growth of online travel agents, providing information about a range of holidays and flights, and inviting potential customers to compare prices, locations and other factors. On the internet, many companies have tried to get customers to sample their information services through push technologies, which place information on potential customers' computers. But there has been a backlash against such pushiness, so other approaches need to be explored.

4 **The usefulness of infomediaries.** In a world of abundant digital information, people and companies want and need to spend less time and money accessing, collecting and using information. Customers online (in common with television and other media) usually have a limited attention span and limited time to search for and use information. The need to focus attention and time on providing the right information at the right time creates an enormous business opportunity for information intermediaries, or infomediaries. On the internet, there are many opportunities to help people find information. Infomediaries focus on providing the information their customers want quickly. This necessitates building a brand reputation based on trust.

Management information systems

Most organisations have their own distinct management information system, providing data for day-to-day operations and decisions that may be arrived at by exercising a degree of "gut feeling". The normal process of collecting, organising, processing, analysing and maintaining information continues routinely. As long as it remains undisturbed, directors and senior managers have the information they need and can have confidence that there are unlikely to be too many surprises (and certainly no serious ones). Unfortunately, few systems are robust enough to cope satisfactorily with dislocating events, such as mergers and acquisitions or major reorganisations. Any event that brings major change will have an impact on the established management information systems. In themselves, such events are often high-risk transitions, requiring high-quality information for their successful management. Changes in information technology and systems, departures of key personnel, new product introductions and organisational change are all likely to dislocate an organisation's management information systems and give rise to insecurity and uncertainty, with major implications for decision-making.

Managers often place undue emphasis on the management information that they receive, dwelling on the details of information collection or storing, rather than focusing on the broader issues of analysis and decision-making. They may request too much information, simply because it is there and is intrinsically interesting rather than relevant. Or they may just see a barrage of data and variables that they ignore or from which they draw out elements that justify their own beliefs or purposes. Achieving balance in the information provided to help decision-makers and support the decisions they make is never easy, and sophisticated management information systems and technology have not made it easier or more effective. Achieving the right balance is something that organisational behaviourists are researching, and it is likely to receive more attention in both business schools and boardrooms. If information is power, how can that power be unlocked and wielded?

The impact of technology on decision-making

The new economy surge of the late 1990s changed people's perceptions of what they could expect in terms of value and customer service. Customers have become more demanding as competitive pressures have increased. But should customers always come first? Or are there times when decisions that adversely affect them may be best? The answer to both questions is yes. Customers are rarely one homogeneous group. Often decisions need to be placed in the context of an overall business approach and choices have to be made. Indeed, there may be several areas where conventional wisdom is being turned on its head with the arrival of new technology, and understanding or auditing the extent of this change may provide some useful insights.

Technology has an immense and diverse impact on business decisions. Adding value, understanding customer needs, assessing costs, being certain of the forces driving profitability and competitive advantage, and enhancing external perceptions of an organisation or brand are all factors that are directly affected by the management and use of information technology. Information and its analysis are crucial to corporate survival and competitive advantage, yet information growth frequently leads to confusion. Coping with the information maze on a daily basis can be a struggle when decisions need to be made quickly and effectively. This is a priority for decision-makers and is addressed further in Chapter 11.

Key questions

- ◪ Do you apply a range of approaches (such as classical, visionary, competitive) to strategic decision-making? Is your approach to decision-making versatile and appropriate in various circumstances?
- ◪ Do managers in the organisation favour one or more styles of decision-making? Are improvements needed in the ways that decisions are made or implemented, or both?
- ◪ What lessons can your organisation learn from the use of technology? In particular, how can technology be used to improve decision-making?
- ◪ How might the application of technology benefit your current and potential competitors?
- ◪ Could the four attributes of internet-derived information listed earlier benefit your organisation?
- ◪ Are your management information systems effective at providing accurate, reliable information when needed? How often are problems identified? Are there checks in place to ensure both the accuracy and security of information?

3 Pitfalls

The way that people think has a fundamental effect on their behaviour and the decisions they make. This chapter examines the most powerful and natural of forces shaping strategic thinking: the human mind.

Everyone has suffered at the hands of a business that does not seem to know what it is doing, or if it does, is doing it badly. There are several types of failure:

- ◪ Thinking flaws, notably the danger of overemphasis.
- ◪ Leadership flaws, resulting in poor management, motivation of people and implementation of decisions.
- ◪ Cultural flaws relating to the organisational environment.

Behavioural flaws

The way that people think, both as individuals and collectively within organisations, affects the decisions that they make in ways that are far from obvious and rarely understood. John Hammond, Ralph Keeney and Howard Raiffa in the *Harvard Business Review*[1] highlighted the fact that bad decisions can often be traced back to the way they were made: the alternatives were not clearly defined; the right information was not collected; the costs and benefits were not accurately weighed. Sometimes the fault lies not in the decision-making process, but in the mind of the decision-maker. The workings of the human brain can lead you towards a number of traps that you will avoid only if you recognise that they exist, and understand which ones are likely to influence your thinking.

Some common traps
The anchoring trap. This is where we give disproportionate weight to the first piece of information we receive. It often happens because the initial impact of the first piece of information is so significant that it outweighs everything else, drowning our ability to effectively evaluate a situation. As a result, the decision (or solution) is anchored on this one issue. To avoid this trap, managers need to be sure about what really is happening, taking care to gather all of the relevant information in order to consider different options.

The status quo trap. This biases us towards maintaining the current situation, even when better alternatives exist. This might be caused by inertia or the potential loss of face if the current position was to change. Managerial recipes – beliefs and approaches that are developed over time from experience and become institutionalised – commonly guide strategic thinking and action. When a business formula worked once, it is convenient to believe that it will do so again. Often there are vested interests in maintaining the status quo. Or people may feel insecure about admitting that things have changed and recognising the need for a new approach. An organisation that as a whole values questioning, experimentation, openness and learning is much less vulnerable to the status quo trap.

The sunk-cost trap. This inclines us to perpetuate the mistakes of the past because we have invested so much in an approach or decision that we cannot abandon it or alter course now. The management accountant's view of this is refreshingly sanguine: if it's spent, it's spent; worry about the present and future, not the past. This trap is particularly significant when managing risk and making investments in new projects or making acquisitions. To avoid it, managers need to plan intelligently and know in advance where the plan can be modified and by how much. Maintaining a clear focus on the desired outcome is crucial, as is keeping a general overview of the project.

The confirming-evidence trap. Also known as confirmation bias, this is when we seek information to support an existing predilection and discount opposing information. It may result from a tendency to seek evidence to justify past decisions or to support the continuation of the current favoured strategy. It can lead managers to fail to evaluate potential weaknesses of existing strategies and to overlook robust alternatives.

A classic example of the confirming-evidence trap is the waiter's dilemma, a thinking flaw that is a self-fulfilling prophecy. Consider a waiter in a busy restaurant. Unable to give excellent service to everyone, he serves only those people that he believes will give a good tip. This appears to work well: only those that he predicts will tip well do so. However, the waiter fails to realise that the good tip may be the result of his actions, and so might the lack of a tip from the other diners. In fact, the only way he can test his judgment is to give poor service to good tip prospects and excellent service to poor tip prospects. Similarly, managers should challenge and test existing assumptions to identify weaknesses in current thinking and to research alternative approaches to strategic development.

The overconfidence trap. Closely linked to the confirming-evidence trap, the overconfidence trap is when people have an exaggerated belief in their ability to understand situations and predict the future. This trap is more subtle and insidious than it may seem: to the overconfident the solution may seem obvious, when in fact a better option lies hidden elsewhere. It is wrong to assume that the best solution to any problem is easily available; because of the unrelenting pace of change, the best solutions often need to be uncovered.

Many factors can cause overconfidence: a lack of sensitivity, complacency (perhaps resulting from past success), a lack of criticism or feedback, a tendency to make assumptions, a confident predisposition or sheer bravado. Confidence is vital for success, particularly with difficult decisions where a steadfast, determined approach is needed. However, it is important to investigate and understand all the options before deciding on the appropriate action. This means not rushing to judgment and avoiding hasty, ill-conceived action. It is also another reason why scenario thinking is valuable.

The framing trap. This is when a problem or situation is incorrectly stated, thus undermining the decision-making process. This is usually unintentional, but not always. Managers habitually follow established, successful formulas (or managerial recipes), and form their views through a single frame of reference. Furthermore, people's roles in an organisation influence the way problems are framed. For example, a manager being judged by the staff turnover in his team is likely to explain the departure of an employee in a way that does not undermine his position. The framing trap often occurs because well-rehearsed and familiar ways of making decisions are dominant and difficult to change. It may lead managers to tackle the wrong problem – decisions may have been reached with little thought and better options may be overlooked. A failure to define the problem accurately may lead either to the wrong solution being implemented or to the right solution being implemented incorrectly.

The causes of the framing trap include poor or insufficient information; a lack of analysis; a feeling that the truth needs to be concealed, or a fear of revealing it; or a desire to show expertise. A simpler cause may be lack of time to frame the problem correctly. Organisations can go out of business if their managers fail to adapt their frame of reference as the business environment changes. Defining problems accurately lays the foundations for solving them. This requires sufficient time, efficient information systems and good analytical skills. It also depends on a supportive atmosphere where matters can be openly discussed.

The recent event trap. Also known as hindsight bias, this trap leads us to give undue weight to a recent (probably dramatic) event or sequence of events. It is similar to the anchoring trap, except it can arise at any time. Research has shown that if an event actually did occur, people often recollect that they had predicted it with a high degree of confidence. Asked about an event that did not occur, they either claimed that they had not predicted it, or that they had placed a low degree of confidence on the prediction of it occurring. Thus we believe that our judgments, predictions and choices are well made, but this confidence may be misplaced.

The prudence trap. This leads us to be overcautious about uncertain factors. It reflects a tendency to be risk averse, and is likely to arise when there is a decision dilemma, when it is felt that to continue with the current approach carries risks and that alternative approaches also carry risks. Yet good decision-making depends on a willingness to take calculated risks and to minimise them. Fear of failure is understandable. Parameters must be set, indicating how and when to manage risk and where experimentation is allowed, and ensuring it is properly managed and controlled.

Coping with decisions
To lower the stress inherent in decision dilemmas, many people avoid a real decision by deciding to wait and see. This may increase risk because it prolongs an outdated and inappropriate strategy. Over-reliance on a previously winning formula has damaged many businesses that were, in their time, successful first-movers. It is dangerous to assume that what has worked before will work again. Putting off real decisions reinforces damaging attitudes and allows time for demotivation and cynicism to take hold. Setting clear strategic priorities can help avoid procrastination, as does empowering people and making their responsibilities clear. The ways that people cope with the stresses of decsion-making include the following:

- Escalation of commitment. Often, when a decision or strategy starts to fail, those responsible commit further resources in an attempt to prove that their previous decisions were right. Escalation of commitment is similar to the sunk-cost trap mentioned earlier.
- Bolstering. This is an uncritical emphasis on one option which often happens when there is no "good" option available, only a choice among the "least worst" courses of action. Bolstering is a way of coping with difficult choices and can result in a sense of invulnerability to external events, especially when it is accompanied by an escalation of commitment. It also results in poor contingency planning in the event that the favoured option falters or fails.
- Shifting responsibility for a difficult decision to another person or group. This is often a sign of weak leadership.

Leadership flaws

More general leadership flaws can also shape strategic decisions:

- Failure of understanding. If you do not properly understand a problem, you are unlikely to find the best solution to it, especially when circumstances are complex or fast-moving. There may be no satisfactory answer, only a choice between competing alternatives that are far from ideal. Information overload can make it difficult to distinguish between cause and effect, and therefore to understand the problem. It can help to ask what is the problem and what is not the problem. Who or what is affected or unaffected by the problem? What is different or unchanged about what is affected?
- Rationalistic planning. This is a similar type of flaw based on the assumption that there is only one effective choice and, therefore, that everyone thinking rationally will arrive at the same conclusion.

Decision-making pitfalls

Cultural flaws

The culture of an organisation can hinder effective strategic decision-making in two opposite ways. Fragmentation occurs when people are in disagreement. Usually, dissent is disguised or suppressed, although it may surface as "passive aggression". Dissent often festers in the background, being muttered to colleagues rather than raised openly. Each fragmented group, and there may be several, is likely to show a confirmation bias and evaluate incoming information to support their initial opinions, rather than view it objectively. Fragmentation may be caused by or be the cause of factionalism and any move to break it may be seen as an attempt to gain dominance by one faction.

Groupthink is when an impression of harmonious agreement is given because ideas that do not support the line a group is taking are suppressed. It may occur because individuals are denied information, or lack the confidence or ability to challenge the dominant views of the group. Close-knit groups may also rationalise the invulnerability of their decisions, inhibiting analysis. The result is an incomplete assessment of available options, and a failure to examine the risks of the decisions that are made. Groupthink can occur when teamwork is either strong or weak. As with fragmentation, the longer it lasts, the more entrenched and "normal" it becomes.

Fragmentation and groupthink stem from a lack of honesty and understanding, and reflect Jerry B. Harvey's Abilene paradox.[2] This concerns a man who suggests a family trip to Abilene, a town in Texas over 50 miles away, on a hot, dry Sunday afternoon. He asks each person in turn if they would like to go, and everyone says yes. However, on the return journey it becomes clear that no one had actually wanted to go. The man's wife agreed to the trip because she thought that her husband was keen to go. The son-in-law agreed because he thought his parents-in-law wanted to go, and the others in the family agreed because they did not want to spoil the trip for everyone else. Even the man who suggested the trip admits that he did so only because he thought that everyone else would prefer to go out rather than stay home.

Such behaviour is common in organisations. Decisions may be validated by people who want to satisfy and support others, or who are keen to avoid conflict and risk. When information is collated and analysed through a filter that reflects a particular perception, the more locked in and self-reinforcing the situation becomes. When such locked-in, self-reinforcing feedback loops exist, there is no chance that the people trapped in them will accurately sense when and why circumstances are changing.

Failure to respond to change

There are numerous examples of businesses that did not sense the need to change, or that failed to deliver the change that was needed and therefore lost a dominant position or went bankrupt. But what about those firms that do manage to change and remain successful, such as Wal-Mart, Royal Dutch/Shell (which have stayed at the top of their industry), the Swedish financial giant Skandia or the Finnish company Nokia (two firms that have dramatically reinvented themselves, the former from a traditional regional bank into a major financial services business and the latter from a wood products company into a mobile phone maker). Responding to the need to change may be complicated by such matters as funding, regulation, customer perceptions and technology, but changing in the right way at the right time is a strategic imperative in today's business environment.

Looking for the emperor's new clothes: Luc Vandevelde and Marks & Spencer

In the 1990s, Marks & Spencer, a leading UK retailer and for a long time one of its most admired companies, fell to ground. Many reasons have been given for the decline, but common to all of the company's woes was a failure to respond to the fast-changing retail market.

Marks & Spencer was established in the late 19th century by Michael Marks, a Russian immigrant, and Tom Spencer, a cashier in a wholesale company that Marks bought following his success in running a market stall in Kirkgate market in Leeds. Growing from a small base, Marks & Spencer had by 1903 become a limited company with capital of £30,000. Both Marks and Spencer died in 1907. Marks's son Simon and his school friend, Israel Sieff, succeeded them, leading the company through the booming 1920s, when demand for clothes rose and the company's market share also increased. In 1926, Marks & Spencer was floated on the stockmarket, valued at £500,000. By 1935, its profits exceeded £1m.

Throughout this growth period, Simon Marks was committed both to respond to change and to engineer it within the company. In 1931, for example, food departments opened in many of Marks & Spencer's 135 stores, establishing a new channel for growth. The destruction of many stores by bombing in the war and the post-war recession led Lord Marks and Lord Sieff, as they had become, to launch Operation Simplification. This was an ambitious plan to cut bureaucracy and staff, paring the business back to its most essential and profitable operations. The decision demonstrated an awareness and willingness to respond to change. The new approach drove much of Marks & Spencer's growth and made it the UK's leading clothes retailer. By 1956, profits exceeded £10m, and in 1962, they topped £25m. Marks & Spencer continued to expand, moving into housewares and financial services. It also opened stores in Europe, Asia and North America.

Under Richard Greenbury, who was both chairman and chief executive, Marks & Spencer's profits topped £1 billion in 1997. But it soon became clear that the company had lost the plot and that the way profits had been squeezed out of the business was not sustainable. A mood of complacency, coupled with Greenbury's autocratic style that left little room for dissent, was not a recipe for good or responsive management. Marks & Spencer's fashion buyers were doing a poor job, and none of the foreign operations was proving successful. But most significant was the way the UK retail market was posing an increasing threat, not least because of new fashion styles and retailing approaches introduced by foreign competitors such as Gap and Zara. Market segmentation had increased competition, reducing market share and profitability.

Marks & Spencer declined because it had gradually and then quickly ceased to be a commercially aware business that was close to the customer, that led rather than followed, that was fleet-footed and that had solid values and standards. It had focused on the short-term bottom line and become institutionally complacent, believing that its position was unassailable.

The solutions
Luc Vandevelde's task when appointed chairman and chief executive was to establish a team capable of managing change and to restore growth and profitability. His approach included:

- **Closing some continental stores** in 2001, placing the business on firmer ground to compete in its chosen (predominantly domestic) markets.
- **Listening to customers**, reinstating the customer focus that had been overshadowed by complacency in the 1990s. This meant doing obvious things like accepting credit cards.
- **Establishing new brands** that would appeal to new types of customers.
- **Aggressive, focused marketing**, showing people how Marks & Spencer had changed. Amazingly, marketing was a relatively new area for the company.
- **Identifying talented people** outside the company to bring into management positions.
- **Managing people more effectively,** restoring a sense of pride and self-worth among employees.

The lessons
- **Anticipate and manage change.** Strategists should always seek to fight on their own terms and on the territory of their choice, using weapons of their own choosing. This means analysing the market intelligently, carefully planning developments, innovating, and maintaining an emphasis on excellence and

customer focus. (This is explored further in Chapter 6.) It is always better to dictate the course of change rather than simply "ride the tiger". This is easier for companies at the top of their industries, such as Microsoft or General Electric, as they are often the dictators of innovation. Market leaders have this power but rarely capitalise on it, which perhaps explains why so many high-profile businesses lose their lustre.

- ☑ **Monitor competitors.** When competitors are strong, it is necessary to deliver an enhanced service or find another way of appealing to customers.
- ☑ **Check the organisational culture and climate.** Continuity is a double-edged sword: it can consistently deliver the business formula that brought success, updating and revitalising it with each new challenge or opportunity, or it can bring complacency and staleness. In Marks & Spencer, senior managers usually rose through the ranks, and the resulting organisational conservatism failed to challenge existing strategies, giving competitors the edge.
- ☑ **Avoid the perils of groupthink and fragmentation.** With his new team, Vandevelde shook up the company so that people pulled together and were encouraged to think for themselves. This had a dramatic impact on profits.
- ☑ **Reduce bureaucracy and streamline decision-making.** Bureaucracy can paralyse. Exacerbated by top-down management, it disconnects different levels of employees. Groupthink can result, as managers feel unable to question or challenge. There is no substitute for getting out and speaking to people, whether they are customers or front-line (and usually well-informed) employees. As John Le Carré, a novelist, said, "A desk is a dangerous place from which to watch the world."

Business survival and success require an understanding of change, as well as the ability to manage it. The combination of understanding and drive that this entails is formidable. Retailing is an uncertain business and prone to sudden change, but Marks & Spencer has adapted to a changed and changing world and has now recovered some lost ground in the process.

Reasons for decline

Many travel agencies have been hit by the growing use of the internet for travel arrangements. Similarly, big airlines have suffered from the competition posed by low cost carriers, compounded by a fear of terrorism. So what prevents organisations from adapting to change successfully? One reason is a lack of effective strategies, in such areas as functional policy, corporate governance and environmental monitoring.

Weak action, combined with poorly timed responses to changing circumstances, can accelerate decline.

Some firms do not realise how their exposure to risk may have changed. Research conducted by Peter Grinyer, David Mayes and Peter McKiernan has identified causes of corporate decline in five main categories:[3]

- Adverse market developments, such as changes in demand or increased competition.
- High cost structure in relation to other sources of competition.
- Weak financial controls often combined with uncertainty about where, when and how to reduce costs, when to spend more, and how much. This is tied in with the sunk-cost trap and risk mismanagement.
- Failure of big projects, with organisations failing to achieve the gains they anticipated. Many dotcom businesses were examples of this, as was Coca-Cola with its disastrous launch of new Coke in the mid-1980s.
- Mergers and acquisitions, which can often be big disappointments, struggling to fulfil their potential. The AOL Time Warner and Daimler Chrysler mergers are two recent examples.

Organisational inertia

The inability to understand change and adapt to it is characterised by organisational inertia. Many organisations falter because they fail to recognise that the market has changed, with increased competition and more organisations offering the same or similar products. It is important that there is a clear, competitive response when:

- competing or substitute products come onto the market;
- technological changes give competitors an advantage or alter customers' preferences;
- substitute products keep prices low and threaten to take current and potential customers;
- products mature, resulting in changes such as reduced prices, market saturation and risk to brand reputation;
- demographic changes occur, including shifts in income distribution;
- social changes take place, for example in fashion tastes;
- demand declines because of a cyclical change – it may be

temporary, but it may be no less damaging for that;

- political developments result in regulatory changes, and possibly the removal of barriers to entry;
- a significant new competitor arrives or emerges;
- rising costs of leaving the market result in intensifying competition, in the face of falling sales;
- product differentiation or a strong cost advantage are lacking.

Overcoming decision-making problems

It may be easy to spot decision-making flaws, particularly in others, but it can be harder to overcome them. The application of common sense is usually a large part of the solution, but two factors need to be taken into account:

- The personal style of the decision-maker and his or her ability to adopt the right approach at the right time.
- The importance of testing and perfecting decisions. For example, scenario planning is valuable in testing and setting strategic decisions; ratio analysis is often valuable when assessing quantitative financial data; simply talking to customers (or employees dealing directly with customers) is valuable if decisions relate directly to customers, and so on.

Some ways of overcoming the barriers to effective decision-making are discussed below.

Being aware (and raising awareness among others)

If you are not aware of a problem, you cannot deal with it; what matters is being honest, open and transparent. It is important that everyone speaks the truth as they see it, without fear of recriminations. If you are in a services business, then providing a better standard of service than your competitors, relative to price, is crucial. If you are in manufacturing or retailing, you must produce or sell things that people want at a price they are willing to pay.

Avoiding subjective or irrational analysis

A lack of objectivity may result from prejudice or being unduly influenced by the halo effect, where past successes blind people to current risks and flaws. It may be connected with false expectations or assumptions about behaviour or circumstances. Or it may be a result of complacency, arrogance, laziness, tiredness or overwork. It can lead to an overestimation of the barriers to entry to your market. Protecting organisational distinctiveness is a frequent advantage, but if it breeds hubris, complacency and an inability to adapt, it is a liability. Decisions and strategies based on perceptions that are no longer valid will be flawed.

A classic example of subjective analysis was IBM's belief in the late 1970s that its pre-eminence in computers and business machines would lead it to dominate the personal computer market. It manufactured the standard computer model and was able to withstand the challenge of competitors such as Apple. However, it failed to realise that being IBM-compatible was only part of the future of this market, and that software that could play on IBM-compatible machines was where real competitive advantage lay. Bill Gates, who realised this, struck a deal with IBM to license his company's operating system to IBM and soon established Microsoft as an industry leader. IBM was left in the comparatively low-margin market of personal computers that it had set out to dominate. In the face of intensifying competition from businesses such as Dell and Compaq, it was ultimately forced to redefine its business in the 1990s as a provider of IT and business consultancy services.

Being sensitive

Failing to appreciate the sensitivity of a situation often makes it worse. Pressures of work, lack of time and too little or too much information are common reasons for people not picking up important nuances. Influencing, leading, communicating, trusting and empowering people can all help to develop and demonstrate awareness. Working out in advance the consequences of decisions is also crucial.

Under its formidable chairman Lord Weinstock, GEC, a UK manufacturing conglomerate, had established an enviable reputation for efficiency and shareholder value, building up a mountain of cash reserves. However, shortly after Lord Weinstock retired, the business refocused its strategy and its cash on moving into the booming telecoms market. Failing to realise that the market was enjoying a short-term boom, it rebranded itself as Marconi, buying at the top of the market, and was then hit by the effects of overcapacity and overvalued businesses and franchises. Marconi's share price was hammered, swiftly losing over 80% of its value. This high-profile disaster happened because the business had failed to display sensitivity to its market, employees or shareholders. Interestingly, many analysts were critical of Lord Weinstock's mountain of cash, and as Marconi, under his successors, spent all the cash and accumulated huge debt in its buying spree, they rated it a really hot stock, until, that is, things started to go wrong.

Establishing clear priorities and objectives

People need to know what to do and how to do it, and they need to have the necessary skills and resources to do it successfully. A lack of focus and direction promotes drift, erodes efficiency and can be very debilitating for an organisation. The example of Jean-Cyril Spinetta's leadership at Air France (see Chapter 2) highlights an approach that emphasised solid, old-fashioned values of service, quality, efficiency and cost control. Despite the travails of the airline industry in recent years, Air France avoided quick-fix or radical solutions, preferring instead reliance on a few clear priorities that its employees could embrace.

Fostering creativity and innovation

Relying on what has worked in the past is no guarantee of success in the future. It is therefore important for an organisation to develop an innovative and creative culture that will help it adapt successfully to change. One way to do this is to question everything about an emerging situation, re-evaluating assumptions that have been made. Also consider whether it is better to look for major leaps forward and visionary breakthroughs, or to adopt an approach emphasising steady, incremental improvement. Richard Branson at Virgin Atlantic attempted to redefine the market for intercontinental air travel with a service that offered a range of innovations, from executive pre-flight chauffeuring to in-flight ice creams. This approach was very much "on brand", exploiting Virgin's reputation as a lively and exciting innovator. The result was to take significant market share on transatlantic routes from its main rival, British Airways.

Understanding substantive issues

A lack of information or analysis, or being overwhelmed by a difficult, sensitive, important or highly complex situation, means that people may waste time on smaller issues, rather than solve the bigger problem. In order to understand the substantive issues you must consider first principles: what is happening and why, what are its consequences, and how can it be resolved? Maintaining a clear focus on the problem-solving process and discussing the situation with others will help develop a sense of perspective.

Focusing on the relevance and potency of the business idea
Many failing organisations lack market and customer focus and do not
have a clear product focus. Regular reviews of strategy and a forward-
looking approach can counter these difficulties.

When IKEA, a Swedish furniture retailer, expanded into North America, it discovered its single approach to selling its products did not work
in this new market – in short, that its business idea was not equally
potent or compelling in different markets. After this lack of initial success, IKEA realised that in North America it had to blend its traditional
Swedish design and low-cost products with specific responses to customer preferences. So it included chests of drawers with deeper drawers, to accommodate more knitwear, and king-sized beds were labelled
in inches rather than centimetres. This led IKEA to source nearly half of
its products in the United States from local suppliers, and nearly one-
third of its total product offerings were designed exclusively for the
American market. This approach has now been more widely adopted,
and in IKEA's recently opened branches in Russia, for example, the products available vary from those sold in other European countries.

Organisational learning and scenarios
There are two increasingly popular approaches to avoiding the pitfalls of
strategic thinking: adaptive organisational learning and scenario thinking.

Adaptive organisational learning is a process of continuous adapta-
tion of behaviour, so that it is better suited to the organisational environment and to improving performance, especially in turbulent times.
Improving efficiency, becoming more effective and innovative in uncertain and dynamic market conditions, allows organisations to learn,
which better equips them for the future. The greater the uncertainty in
the environment, the greater is the need for fast learning, as this enables
a fast and effective response. Arie De Geus, former head of group planning at Royal Dutch/Shell, argues that an organisation's ability to learn
faster than its competitors is the ultimate source of competitive advantage.[4] He outlines several aspects of learning:

- experimentation at the periphery (piloting);
- taking time to perceive the nature of developments;
- reflecting on experience;
- developing "theories of action"; and
- acting on the conclusions reached.

Scenarios are effective because they enable decision-makers to examine a wide range of information, to understand what is driving the present and the future, and to challenge their assumptions as to how and why the future may evolve. The outcome is a deeper understanding of alternative views and a new language and method that promote flexible and responsive organisations. Challenging mental models and orthodoxy leads to shared understanding and effective joint action.

Scenario thinking, or what Kees van der Heijden terms the "strategic conversation", is a process divided into two parts: a formal element designed by managers, revolving around planning cycles and quantitative information, and an informal part, characterised by casual "corridor" conversations. The latter is neither designed nor controlled by managers, and is usually qualitative and anecdotal in nature. In *Scenarios: The Art of Strategic Conversation*,[5] Van der Heijden states:

> *It is extremely relevant, because it determines where people's attention is focused. These conversations influence and are influenced by the mental models which have developed over time, and which determine how individuals inter-subjectively see the world, how they interpret events, how they discriminate and decide what is important and what is not.*

Whatever scenarios are developed, none may come out exactly as outlined. But that is not the point. Scenario thinking is principally concerned with the quality of analysis and thinking in an organisation: identifying causes of change and emphasising the ability to learn and adapt.

Key questions

Decision-making flaws are common in every organisation. To assess and improve decision-making capabilities, consider the extent to which the hidden traps of decision-making hamper the organisation. Do people:

- Give disproportionate weight to the first piece of information they receive?
- Seek to maintain the status quo?
- Pursue failing decisions, in a forlorn attempt to recover past investments and credibility?
- Seek confirming evidence to justify past or present decisions?

- Display overconfidence?
- Display excessive caution?
- Incorrectly frame or state an issue, often leading to a flawed decision?
- Give undue weight to a recent or dramatic event?
- Procrastinate, delaying important decisions?

As well as these common problems and behaviours, strategic decision-making in groups is often hampered by groupthink and fragmentation.

- To what extent do these approaches affect decisions?
- How prepared is your organisation to respond to change? Can you recall examples when the company has driven change, responded to it, or failed to do either? What are the reasons for this failure?
- What is the solution? (The best and simplest approach is to understand the root causes and then confront them, although this may often mask a complex and sensitive, even explosive, situation.)

4 Rational or intuitive? Frameworks for decision-making

The rational approach

For decision-makers, the significance of their decisions is inversely proportional to the number that they make; typically, senior executives make only a few, important decisions. It therefore matters especially that strategic decisions which will have a significant impact are intelligently and soundly made and thoroughly and effectively implemented. Peter Drucker believes that to achieve this requires a rational approach to decision-making, relying on a set of sequential steps that lead to successful decisions. He argues that:

> *Every decision is a risk-taking judgment ... Effective executives try to make the few important decisions on the highest level of conceptual understanding. They try to find the constants in a situation, to think through what is strategic and generic rather than to "solve problems". They are, therefore, not overly impressed by speed in decision-making; rather, they consider virtuosity in manipulating a great many variables a symptom of sloppy thinking. They want to know what the decision is all about and what the underlying realities are which it has to satisfy. They want impact rather than technique. And they want to be sound rather than clever.*[1]

There are many rational, methodical and sequential approaches to decision-making. This rational route is seen as providing a framework for reaching an effective decision and involves the following:

- Assessing the situation
- Defining the critical issues
- Specifying the decision
- Making the decision
- Implementing the decision
- Monitoring the decision and making adjustments as events unfold

Assessing the situation

Rational decision-makers start by asking whether the decision relates to a permanent, underlying or structural issue, or whether it is the result of an isolated event. Some decisions are generic and are best addressed with a consistent rule or principle; isolated events are exceptional and are best resolved when they arise. Furthermore, a response depends on the particular features of each situation. What may appear to be an isolated event is often an early indicator of a generic problem. Product-quality problems are usually in this category, with a particular failure traced back to a faulty process or poor morale. Typically, such generic problems are identified only after a lengthy period of investigation and analysis.

When Enron and its auditors Andersen were identified as having misled people about the energy corporation's financial position, this was initially seen as an isolated problem. Subsequently, lax accounting standards were seen as a generic issue, requiring action from regulators. With such a generic issue, the response needs to be consistent: a rule, policy or principle is required. Contrast this to the situation faced by firms such as Lego, a Danish toymaker established in the 1930s. Its building bricks became established worldwide as a favourite toy for children, yet when their popularity declined it was at first unclear whether this was a specific reaction against Lego or a result of a generic move away from "learning" toys to more action-oriented children's entertainment. Lego found that there was no generic move against its products; the decrease in popularity was a reaction to a brand that was seen as tired and increasingly irrelevant. Its solution was to open theme parks, alter its product range and brand its products with films and other forms of entertainment.

When an organisation faces something that is new to it but that has been experienced by others, the response requires a blend of standard best-practice techniques and an appraisal of what is distinctive about the circumstances faced. When Microsoft was indicted for antitrust practices this was a first for the firm, but others had already been in that position. When an organisation is in the eye of a press and public relations storm for the first time, it is important to recognise and understand both the unique attributes of the situation and the general principles that can be applied. Microsoft needed to find specific counter-arguments to the Justice Department's case, but it also needed to follow standard procedures for organisations that are being indicted. It needed to get its case across to customers through the media and to seek support from influential people and organisations, using tried and tested techniques.

Decision-makers are rarely faced with issues or events that are genuinely unique. Applying standard rules in exceptional circumstances is unlikely to succeed, however. It could be said to be the exception that proves the rule.

Defining the critical issues

When considering a decision, among the aspects to be defined and examined are the critical issues, who or what is affected, likely developments, the timescale involved, sensitive issues, as well as previous, comparable situations. In short, all the relevant issues should be considered. A partial analysis is almost as bad as no analysis at all, as it gives an ill-founded confidence and legitimacy to the decision. This view is emphasised by Drucker, writing in the *Harvard Business Review*:

> *Effective decision-makers always test for signs that something atypical or unusual is happening, always asking: Does the definition explain the observed events, and does it explain all of them? They always write out what the definition is expected to make happen ... and then test regularly to see if this really happens. Finally, they go back and think the problem through again whenever they see something atypical, when they find unexplained phenomena, or when the course of events deviates, even in details, from expectations.*[2]

Funnelling is a useful, methodical and rational technique. This involves collecting as much information and data as possible and reducing it to the principal issues through a process of prioritising and elimination.

Two common mistakes beset decision-making. The first is to react to a situation as if it were a unique series of events, when the problem it reflects is a generic one requiring the application of a consistent rule, principle or strategy. This results from an inability to see the big picture or to understand where the events might lead. The second is to perceive a situation as if it were a generic issue requiring an old solution; if it is a new type of situation, a new solution is required.

Looking for the right route: Chrysler's return

During the late 1980s, Chrysler's sales in America and abroad were weakening. Critics claimed that the organisation was uninspired and lagging behind its competitors. Each problem was seen as unique and people tackled them separately, whereas they were really symptoms of a larger problem facing the whole company. The solution for Chrysler was to see the bigger picture, thus rescuing the company's fortunes. Bob Lutz, the company's president, believed the answer was to develop an innovative, exciting car. Stylish, with a powerful ten-cylinder engine and five-speed manual transmission, the Dodge Viper was given a premium price of $50,000. Many advised that no American-made car would sell in volume at that price and that the investment would be better spent elsewhere. Lutz's idea was based on nothing more than personal instinct, without any significant market research. He had to overcome considerable internal opposition, as this approach to decision-making was not typical at Chrysler. However, the Dodge Viper was a massive commercial success. It changed the public's perception of Chrysler, halted the company's decline and boosted morale.

Lutz's belief that producing the radically different Dodge Viper was the right decision for Chrysler has been hailed as a triumph of instinct over rationality. Yet it could be claimed that the decision was entirely rational. When threatened with stagnating sales, a lacklustre brand and competitive pressures, what else was there to do but throw the rulebook away, innovate and connect with customers by "wowing" them?

Lutz may have reached his decision through instinct, but it was influenced by experience, which told him which rules to apply.

Specifying the decision

The next step is to define what the decision must achieve. Every decision should have a minimum set of goals: rules to comply with, a timescale for completion and a method of execution. This helps to ensure focus and smooth implementation. Having a clear specification can prevent changes that would undermine the decision, and it can help when the original decision needs to be adapted because of changing circumstances. Potential conflicts need to be clearly understood, monitored and where necessary resolved; if they are not, the potential for failure is considerable.

Making the decision

Decisions often involve compromise, and as long as the essential goals will still be achieved there is nothing wrong with this. Sometimes the ideal solution is unattainable, but it is better to have 50% of something than 100% of nothing.

It is important to know what the effect of a compromise will be. However, worrying too much from the start about what is acceptable and achievable may lead to compromises being made too easily. Always have a clear view of the ideal decision, and then test it. If compromise is necessary, make sure it is made positively, with a clear focus on what needs to be achieved.

In this stage of the process, creativity and innovation will help to uncover the most effective solution and to ensure that it is implemented successfully.

Implementing the decision

Understanding what needs to be achieved – defining the decision – is usually the most difficult part of the process. It should be made as inclusive as possible and result in a clear commitment. However, executing the decision is usually the most time-consuming, critical phase. It involves the following:

- Planning how it will be implemented. There is no point in arriving at a good decision if you go on to implement it in a way that does not work.
- Delegating and clearly assigning responsibility for specific tasks. This entails building confidence, checking understanding, coaching and mentoring, as well as structuring the organisation so that people are best positioned to carry out their tasks.
- Communicating with people. It is important to ensure that all those involved know what the decision is and understand and support it. This includes people who may seem to be on the periphery but are influencers (confidants and mentors) of those executing it. Their support is essential.
- Motivating, mobilising and rewarding those taking the decision. To ensure that the standards for accomplishing the decision are clear and changed if needed, it is important to provide incentives; remuneration, recognition and status can often mobilise people to succeed.
- Managing resources so that the people carrying out the

decision have the necessary equipment to complete their task.

Monitoring and making adjustments

There are two certainties in decision-making: the people who make and implement decisions are fallible; and the context in which decisions are implemented will be subject to change. So implementation must be monitored to ensure that information management and reporting procedures are built into the process. By itself, this is not enough: reports, written information and communications are often unable to convey the complexity of issues. Management by walking about (MBWA) is a useful, if surprisingly rare, technique. There is no substitute for seeing how things are going, or getting a trusted subordinate to look. This is a fundamental method in the military, where decisions are inspected not because people are distrusted or need supervision, but because of the dangers of poor or misunderstood communications. In the view of Robert Townsend, CEO of Avis:

> All decisions should be made as low as possible in the
> organisation. The charge of the Light Brigade was ordered by
> an officer who wasn't there looking at the territory.

Emails and phone calls can appear to take the place of visiting the people implementing the decision. They cannot. Moreover, people can be lulled into a false sense of security. Personal involvement is a chance to motivate and encourage, as well as an opportunity to see where adjustments will or may be necessary as circumstances change. A technique that can help to manage information and monitor this part of the process is the concept of "information orientation" outlined by Donald Marchand and explained in Chapter 11. This approach highlights the importance of aligning an organisation's information management practices and its behaviours and values, as well as technology, to ensure that it is informed, flexible and responsive.

Decision-making is a cycle (see Figure 4.1); monitoring necessarily leads back to the assessment stage. After all, assessment of future decisions should start with the monitoring of current ones.

The intuitive approach

Instinct and its impact on rational decision-making

Making a decision and implementing it can be messy. No matter how much planning and preparation take place, the process is often confusing,

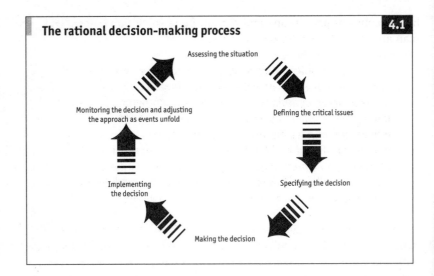

The rational decision-making process

4.1

Assessing the situation

Monitoring the decision and adjusting
the approach as events unfold

Defining the critical issues

Implementing
the decision

Specifying the decision

Making the decision

fast-moving and uncertain, and therefore tense and unsettling. It is comforting to think of decision-making as a rational, methodical and ordered process, but the reality is different. Events are not always ordered or clear and the relevant information may be unavailable, making it more difficult to classify, define, specify and arrive at a decision that will be effective. People do not always think in a consistently ordered way, as the thinking flaws described in Chapter 3 show. This undermines the reliability of a rational approach and points to the need to combine it with an instructive or intuitive approach. The rational approach provides a framework for action, ensuring that nothing is omitted, pitfalls are avoided and best-practice techniques are applied. The intuitive approach provides the inspiration, insight and instinct needed to identify and explore the best options.

Rationality provides the outer framework, together with important milestones and techniques; intuition provides the detail and ingenuity. Creativity and sensitivity ensure optimum conditions for success, where the best choices are offered, selected and implemented. As the Chrysler example referred to earlier in this chapter shows, instinct, within the framework of the decision-making process, produces breakthrough thinking.

The role of instinct in complex, ambiguous or urgent decisions
Decisions are complex and ambiguous. They are concerned with choices, rather than absolute situations of right or wrong, reducing the role of quantitative methods. Making the right decision is made harder

by the constant pace, scope and depth of change. Ralph Larsen, chairman and CEO of Johnson & Johnson, says:

> Very often, people will do a brilliant job up through middle management levels, where it's very heavily quantitative in terms of decision-making. But then they reach senior management, where the problems get more complex and ambiguous, and we discover that their judgment or intuition is not what it should be, it's a big problem ... Often there is absolutely no way that you could have the time to thoroughly analyse every one of the options or alternatives available to you, so you have to rely on your business judgment.[3]

People have an innate ability to handle complexity and to examine issues critically. Sound judgment, instinct and experience, combined with the confidence to act, are precisely what decision-makers need. Technology, prolonged discussion and quantitative methods can be unnecessary or a waste of time. The instinctive approach works best in softer business areas such as marketing, public relations and communication, managing people and researching. Areas such as planning, process management and finance are harder business functions that benefit from an analytical approach. Although the softer areas still benefit from information and measurement, an instinctive, intuitive approach can save time and resources: providing, of course, that the decision is right.

Instinct and intuition are valuable forms of tacit knowledge
The mind is continuously processing information subconsciously. Henry Mintzberg believes that revelation occurs when the conscious mind realises something that the subconscious mind already knew. This validates the instinctive approach. Intuition is a tacit form of knowledge, complementing rather than undermining the rational approach to decision-making.

Emotions filter and guide decisions
Decisions are guided by our emotions in various ways. Emotions act as filters, prioritising information and provoking a physical response to influences, from laughter to stress. The mind sets the agenda during decision-making through the filter of emotional responses. It is important to know how to manage emotion and instinct effectively, as they provide a clear sense of priority, understanding of intangibles and determination.

Although they can be flawed, they can also provide the spark of creativity, the flash of insight and the strength to pursue the best course. This view is outlined by Alden Hayashi, writing in the *Harvard Business Review*:

> *Decision-making is far from a cold, analytic process ... Instead, our emotions and feelings play a crucial role by helping us filter various possibilities quickly, even though our conscious mind might not be aware of the screening. Our intuitive feelings thus guide our decision-making to the point at which our conscious mind is able to make good choices. So just as an abundance of emotion (anger, for example) can lead to faulty decisions, so can its paucity.[4]*

Instinct and pattern recognition are keys to analysis and creativity

Instinct provides a rich resource for managers. Effective analysis depends on seeing the links between various data and then interpreting the patterns. Rational techniques, such as brainstorming and reversal theory, can help, but an ability to see patterns cannot be achieved by rationality alone. Herbert Simon, professor of psychology and computer science at Carnegie Mellon University, believes that experience enables people to group information so that they can store, retrieve and apply it. As he argues:

> *Experts see patterns that elicit from memory the things they know about situations ... We found that what distinguishes experts is that they have very good encyclopedias that are indexed, and pattern recognition is that index.*

The ability to perceive patterns across data and subjects is what distinguishes exceptional decision-makers from good ones. Instinct brings with it the ability to cross-refer, to see things laterally and from a different perspective. It also brings into play ideas, insights and experience from a multitude of sources. These enable people to:

- recognise and understand situations and issues quickly;
- apply experience, ideas and techniques from one field of experience to another;
- prioritise actions effectively;
- sense emerging difficulties, and to build confidence and urgency.

The benefits of pattern recognition provided by the instinctive approach can be immense.

Instinct and rationality are both flawed

Just as instinct, intuition and emotion can result in a biased, irrational and flawed judgment, an overemphasis on rationality can lead to subconscious knowledge, experience and insight being ignored. Both need to be kept in balance. In the words of Michael Eisner, for many years CEO of the Walt Disney Company: "Balanced emotions are crucial to intuitive decision-making." Many difficulties, such as overconfidence, can be traced back to a flawed, unbalanced application of either the rational or instinctive approach.

Balanced emotions and bounded rationality are both needed for decisions to succeed. The rational approach provides a check on the application of instinct, which can run away in a flurry of creativity, excitement and emotion. Similarly, a balanced instinct counteracts the sterile, uniform structure of the rational approach. Instinct, intuition and emotion are resources that can be used to bring flair and insight, leading to the best decisions. It is also worth considering that unique human instinct provides a valuable commodity in business: scarcity. And scarcity often determines value.

Key questions

- Are managers in your organisation comfortable with using the rational approach to decision-making, and do they feel able to trust their intuition?
- Are there any decisions that could have been improved with either greater rationality or more confidence in intuition? Can these serve as examples of areas needing improvement?
- Is the organisation too bureaucratic for intuitive, flexible and swift decision-making? How might the intuition and expertise of people in the organisation be used?
- Are decisions made close to the action, their point of execution, or are they made some distance away? Has this caused difficulties or could it in future?
- What are the most important decisions currently facing the organisation? How are they being resolved, and who is responsible?
- Which decisions arising over the next three years will be the most significant? What planning is being done to resolve these?
- What do your customers, employees and shareholders think of the organisation's ability to make the right decisions? How do they feel that the situation could improve?

2
MAKING IT HAPPEN: CONCEPTS AND TOOLS
FOR STRATEGIC DECISION-MAKING

5 Making strategic decisions

There are many approaches to taking the strategic decisions that affect the direction and performance of an organisation or team. This chapter examines the ideas, old and new, that benefit decision-makers. Some provide a ready framework for action and others offer insights that can be readily applied. Often a combination of methods is the best approach in dealing with the changing business environment.

Reversal theory

> We are not always the same: we are inconsistent, we develop and we change, and so too do the people that we need to influence or lead. We are different people at different times, even under the same circumstances. This is important to understand if we are to successfully work with others and build effective relationships.

So says Michael Apter, a professor of psychology at Georgetown University in the United States.[1] Reversal theory is a prominent theory of motivation, the acceptance of which is increasing among businesses and other organisations. It resulted from work started in the mid-1970s by Ken Smith, a professor of psychology, and Apter, who developed it further.

How it works

At the heart of the theory is the idea that our experience is shaped by alternative ways of seeing the world. Specifically, four pairs of opposite states have been discerned and we "reverse" between these opposites in our everyday life. In this way, reversal theory recognises the paradoxes of human behaviour, suggesting that all individuals are:

◪ motivated to be serious and pursue goals, but also to play, take risks and look for excitement;
◪ motivated to conform, but also to challenge;
◪ motivated by issues of mastery (of people, processes and ideas) but also by notions of sympathy (caring, friendship and affection);
◪ motivated by interest and focus on themselves, but also on others.

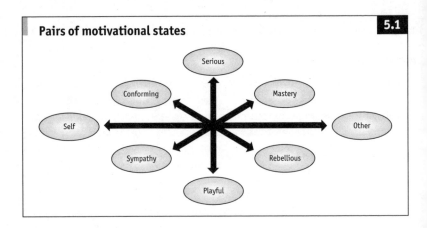

Pairs of motivational states 5.1

Serious · Conforming · Mastery · Self · Other · Sympathy · Rebellious · Playful

Each of these statements encapsulates two motivational states, or ways in which we view situations. At different times we can see the same activity in quite different ways. Although the activity is the same, our response to it changes because our motivational state changes. Figure 5.1 shows the four pairs of opposite states that we switch or reverse between. These combine with each other in various ways at different times to give rise to the full range of human emotions and behaviour. There are eight basic motives, each representing a motivational state. Having them on opposite sides of the circle represents the fact that they are in opposition.

The basic insight is that it is in the nature of human beings to be complex and inconsistent. We are different people at different times, even under the same circumstances. Experiences are shaped by a set of alternative ways of seeing the world. Behaviour reverses between the four pairs of opposite states. Understanding and managing these inconsistencies improves decision-making and performance. Proponents of reversal theory believe that it is important to understand this if we are to work with others, build effective relationships and make successful decisions.

Because we experience all eight of these states with differing amounts of time spent in each, and as every state has something positive to offer, managers should endeavour to exploit the full range of motivational states. Five things determine the way we make decisions.

1 **Opposite psychological needs.** Psychological needs are opposite and contrasting.[2] For instance, the need for serious achievement is contrary

Table 5.1 **Contribution of motivational states to organisational behaviour**

Motivational state	Characteristics
Serious ...	➡ Serious, goal-oriented, prefers planning ahead. Focus on achievement and direction. Risk conscious, anxiety-avoiding.
... or playful	➡ Focus on experimenting, creativity and open thinking: intrinsic pleasure of the activity or the job itself.
Conformist ...	➡ Focus on implementation, following agreements and processes. Concerned with fitting-in, keeping to the rules, following convention.
... or rebellious	➡ Focus on being different, breaking conventions, critical analysis and conflict. Independent, unconventional.
Mastery ...	➡ Wanting the team or the organisation to succeed. Focus on building up the power and resources of others.
... or sympathy	➡ Care-oriented, sees life as co-operative, sensitive, supportive, positive and empathic.
Self-oriented ...	➡ Focus on personal success, willing to take responsibility, control and master new challenges.
... or other-oriented	➡ Focus on emotionally supporting and caring for others, team spirit, building harmony and good personal working relations, wanting to belong and co-operate. Identifies with others.

to the need for playfulness, doing things for their own sake. Steve Carter, managing director of Apter International, describes reversal theory as follows:

> *Psychologically healthy people require each of these contrasting psychological needs to be satisfied, and this is achieved by frequently switching – reversing – between them. This means that people are inherently inconsistent, even self-contradictory. This inconsistency is to be expected – more than that, it is desirable for a full and psychologically healthy life.*

The potential implications are significant: understanding one's own and others' motivational state promotes successful decision-making.

2 **Motivational style.** Psychological needs are part of a general way of seeing the world, interpreting experience and acting. Their opposite nature gives rise to contrasting motivational styles.

3 **Dominant motivational styles.** Consistencies do exist, as an individual is generally one kind of person or another over time. But although a state can dominate, it is not exclusive. Thus someone may tend towards the playful style, although the opposite serious style will surface occasionally.

4 **Determining key styles.** Typically, one or two styles determine behaviour at any one moment, with the other styles organised around them in a supportive or less important role. These pivotal styles represent an individual's key styles.

5 **The four domains of experience.** Reversal theory points to four domains of experience:

- The means-ends domain (serious versus playful), in which we are aware of having some purpose and engaging in some activity towards achieving that purpose. This purposefulness gives what we are doing meaning.
- The rules domain (conforming versus rebellious), in which we are concerned with things that govern what we do and are allowed to do, such as expectations, conventions, routines, etiquette, the status quo and so on.
- The transactions domain (mastery versus sympathy), in which we interact in a particular way.
- The relationships domain (self-oriented versus other-oriented), in which we are concerned with our relationship with the person or organisation we are doing something for or with.

The crux of the theory is that within each domain there are two opposite ways of experiencing that domain. Although individuals are aware of all of them to different degrees at the same time, one may be more prominent.

Implications of reversal theory
There are several implications of reversal theory for the way that decisions are made.

1 **Does the end or the means drive decisions?** It is usually clear when making a decision that sometimes the end is important and sometimes the means matter most. Some activities may be embarked upon because the means of getting to the end are necessary or valuable. Indeed, there may not even be an end; the activity may be just part of a continuing process. Other decisions may be undertaken because the end is highly desirable, even if the means are not enjoyable. Understanding whether it is the means or the ends that matter, can help to clarify the best choice or decision.

2 **Should you conform or rebel?** The rules domain highlights the contrast between conforming and rebelling or challenging. Seeing a decision in these terms can help to clarify options. Is it a time to play safe and conform, or should you be looking for a radical new option? Frustration can result because in the conforming state we may feel constricted, whereas in the rebellious state we want to change and be different. The solution is to decide which motivational state is needed and to bring it into play when making the decision.

3 **How much control is desirable?** The transactions domain highlights two fundamentally different aspects to interactions. The mastery motivational state is all about power: being in charge, winning, feeling strong. In contrast, the sympathy motivational state is about caring, in which friendship and sensitivity are paramount. Again, it is important to understand which state is appropriate and most likely to deliver a successful decision, and then to enter that state.

4 **How much do relationships matter?** In the relationships domain, if the outcome of an action is judged primarily in terms of how it affects the individual, it is the self-oriented motivational state. If the outcome is judged primarily in terms of how it affects something or someone else, it is the other-oriented state. Some decisions benefit from a gut instinct, being made by individuals with faith in themselves or sufficient dynamism to act in isolation from others. Other decisions require a much more associative, collaborative style, gathering views, ideas or commitment from others. It is important to understand which approach is most effective and appropriate. As Carter explains:

> *We spend our lives moving between these different*
> *motivational states or styles, producing ever-changing*

> *kaleidoscopes of state combinations. When one changes from one state to its opposite, this takes place all at once. It is not a gradual process, but one that immediately goes to completion.*

Many people view the ability to recognise this flux of states in themselves and others as increasingly useful when formulating and implementing decisions.

Operational business decisions

Successful operational business decisions can be achieved by:

- Managing knowledge and information
- Getting the corporate culture right
- Fostering creativity and innovation
- Focusing on continuous improvement
- Empowering and mobilising people
- Fitting operational decisions with the overall strategy

Managing knowledge and information systems

Establishing systems that routinely provide accurate, reliable information is essential. Organisations need to exploit all knowledge, from information held on computers to the expertise and experience of their employees, to ensure that durable, effective decisions are made. Examples of businesses that manage to do this well include logistics firms, which provide customers with up-to-the-minute information about the location of their parcels, and online bookstores which build up an understanding of their customers' reading tastes. However, not all knowledge systems need to be computerised. Law firms and professional practices generally are good at getting to know their clients, storing large amounts of useful information, usually in the heads of the partners, about their clients and their interests. This knowledge is certainly no less legitimate or valuable for being held outside a computer system. What matters is that it is shared and used, and this relies on the culture of the organisation.

Getting the corporate culture right

Corporate culture directly affects the quality and effectiveness of decisions, both what is decided and how it is implemented. The difficulty is that corporate culture is subject to innumerable different influences. As a result, it should be managed by:

- defining the vision and mission;
- setting the overriding values;
- leading by example;
- treating others as you would wish to be treated; and
- building a positive, blame-free environment in which all issues can be discussed without ridicule or hostility.

Fostering creativity and innovation

Building competitive advantage is not only about doing your best to attract and satisfy customers; it is also about attracting and satisfying them more than the competition does. This invariably requires decisions to be innovative, that is, cleverer than those of the competition. To do this, an organisation must encourage challenges to accepted norms and engage in direct dialogue with customers and other stakeholders. It should not rely on assumptions that have little evidence to support them. Having a corporate culture that encourages or allows this is essential. In reversal theory terms, the rebellious motivational state, rather than the conforming state, needs to dominate.

Focusing on continuous improvement

Continuous improvement through a commitment to learning, development and investment will often help to keep operational decisions incisive and relevant. Past performance and areas of weakness must be regularly assessed. A commitment to developing individuals, training people and spreading best-practice techniques is also necessary. An organisation must be prepared to challenge established systems and processes, and to set new targets in its pursuit of improved performance.

Empowering and mobilising people

For decisions to be formulated accurately and implemented effectively, people must have the freedom to act and to be able to exploit their potential. This requires the removal of unnecessary bureaucratic or procedural constraints, giving people clear (and possibly expanding) areas of responsibility and authority. The quality and ultimately the success of strategic decisions will be profoundly influenced by people's level of motivation. Thus their efforts need to be mobilised and focused, and recognised and rewarded, in such a way that they tackle the important issues affecting the success of the business with commitment and determination.

Fitting operational decisions with overall strategy

A strategic plan should guide actions and decisions, providing a sense of purpose, energy and direction. It should also offer a means of communicating, motivating and co-ordinating efforts throughout an organisation, helping to focus on areas for improvement or development. A strategic plan provides an opportunity to change an organisation's nature: its purpose, its activities and even its organisational culture, including values and the ways things are done. It can embrace a set of guiding principles as well as a practical framework for achieving its aims. It also offers a means by which performance can be measured and assessed. So how can strategic plans be made to guide and direct operational decisions? The following course of action outlines some necessary steps.

- Subdivide strategic plans into a business plan for each operating unit, and then into objectives for each department, team and ultimately each individual. Always start by asking some basic questions such as: What business are we in? What is our purpose? Where are we now? Where do we want to be in the future? How will we achieve this?
- Consult widely to identify opportunities and decide priorities. Innovation and common-sense ideas come from employees at the lowest level as well as the highest and from customers and suppliers.
- Assess the organisation's competitive position. Current trends need to be taken into account, to highlight strengths and weaknesses.
- Focus on the purpose of the organisation. What does it do? What makes it unique? Does it need to change? What will help to achieve success in the future? Take a balanced view of the opportunities. Too narrow a perspective may result in missed opportunities; too broad a canvas can make it difficult to focus, bringing risks and learning curves associated with diversification.
- Communicate a powerful vision. This should include a clear statement of what the organisation's business is, where it is going and how it will get there. A vision or mission statement must be inspirational and help win commitment. It must also be realistic, understandable and clearly understood by everyone in the organisation.
- Set time frames. Vision statements are concerned with the long

term, but the strategic planning process must provide objectives that are attainable within a time frame of 1–5 years. Without short-term goals to aim for, it is difficult to maintain momentum and motivation.

- ▨ Set clear objectives. The most effective managers translate a vision into practical objectives, taking account of the strengths and weaknesses of the people they manage.
- ▨ A strategic plan cannot be static. It must be adaptable to change and must reflect the process of continuous improvement and development within an organisation. To keep the plan relevant and realistic, it is essential to evaluate and modify it on a rolling basis, mindful of changing circumstances and new opportunities or problems.

Decisions that involve legal issues
In dealing with legal issues, there are a number of guiding principles.

Identify vulnerabilities
It is important to assess the areas of greatest vulnerability: particular contract terms, employment or regulatory issues, laws relating to advertising and data protection, or whatever. Once these have been identified, the level of vulnerability should be assessed and then monitored closely, taking steps to establish necessary training and compliance.

Never ignore or trivialise legal action
A threat of legal action may be tactical, but it should always be taken seriously and, wherever possible, anticipated so that preventive measures can be taken. If the worst happens and the organisation is faced with legal action, even though, according to the International Bar Association, over 90% of cases never reach court, large amounts of time and money may have to be spent dealing with the matter. It may also mean that projects have to be delayed or products withdrawn from sale until the matter is resolved.

Seek legal advice and early resolution
Taking legal advice early on may save a great deal of time and expense later. It can also help to avoid undermining your case, either through ill-advised action or ignorance of the legal implications. Negotiating "without prejudice" allows all concerned to explore different options to resolve the situation, as any offers cannot subsequently be revealed in

court. At this stage, gather the relevant documentation, in case the case does go to court.

Prepare

If legal action ensues, review your options and consider any implications. The legal team should possess decision-making authority in internal and external commercial communication issues and technical legal decisions. It is important to clearly define the rights and wrongs of the case, identifying where the organisation is on firm ground and where it is weak. This can also help to identify where compromise is possible. Where it is not, endeavour to understand what the other party wants to achieve. Then negotiate with a view to settling the matter out of court.

Settling

Once a dispute is settled, taking time to reflect when the heat is off will help provide an understanding of what happened, and why, and how it can be avoided in the future. It is worth making a written evaluation to help inform future decisions.

Problem solving

A problem solving process

A hidden trap within problem solving is the danger of overanalysis, when often what is really required is nothing more than a pen, paper and a period of quiet thought and discussion. The following points are important in all problem-solving styles.

1 **Identifying the problem.** What is the nature of the problem? What is its importance to your operations? Asking or answering these questions sets the tone for how the problem is tackled (for example, whether it is handled urgently or patiently, individually or collectively).

2 **Collecting and processing information.** What information is needed to solve the problem, what data are available, and what extra information may be required? Too little information may make it difficult to come up with a solution. Too much information may make it difficult to see what the solution is.

3 **Generating possible solutions.** Set an exploratory tone to the problem-solving process. This will allow a range of potential solutions to be generated.

4 **Assessing options.** Generate certain criteria (financial, time, organisational precedent and workability) against which different courses of action can be rated. This helps to determine which approach is best.

5 **Making the decision and informing people.** Once a solution has been determined, it should be communicated clearly to all those responsible for implementing it or to those affected by it in order to counter any confusion.

6 **Implementing the solution.** Set a time frame for delivery and deadlines for each stage. After this, it is a matter of seeing that everything is done on time and that the inevitable glitches in the implementation process are overcome.

7 **Verifying the decision.** When the plan has been implemented, its effects can be monitored to see if they are what was desired, or whether they have resulted in other problems that will need solving.

These steps are common to all forms of problem solving, but there are many ways to complete them. Some problems may require ingenious solutions that can only be arrived at by the careful adoption of such different techniques as ratio analysis and brainstorming. It is therefore necessary to differentiate between two types of problem: programmed and non-programmed.

- **Programmed problems** are usually those that occur as a routine part of a manager's job. Even when they are complex, requiring careful deliberation, the solutions are often found by following organisational precedent and procedures. Examples include machine breakdown, salary and staff dilemmas, and budget issues. Linear programming, queuing theory and decision-tree techniques are methods that can be used to deal with such problems.
- **Non-programmed problems** are those for which there is no single system or procedure for determining the right course of action. They may involve anything from new-product development to the shape of a marketing campaign, and they are usually of fundamental importance to the success of particular product lines, even an organisation itself. The most common but not always the most effective technique for solving non-

programmed problems is creative problem solving, including brainstorming. Other useful techniques include cause and effect analysis and Pareto analysis.

Techniques for problem solving

Cause and effect analysis. When treating a patient, a doctor observes the symptoms to decide what the problem is. Similarly, in cause and effect analysis, one first determines the effects of the problem in order to work out what the actual problem is and deal with it. To do this, it helps to take the following steps.

- ◪ Label the problem. Express its effects in detail so that others can also identify what it is. Labels should endeavour to connect effects to possible causes. For example, if the effect is a 10% increase in late deliveries of goods in the last month, then connect this to all the causes of this problem, such as people, poor transport, inefficient order systems, limited product availability, or whatever.
- ◪ Identify the root causes of the problem. The most common are likely to be people, materials and equipment. For example, if late product delivery is because of poor communication, then communications systems or bureaucracy might be the root cause. A flow diagram of work processes can help to illustrate the relationship between problems, their effects and their causes.
- ◪ Collect data on the causes of the problem. Asking the staff involved for their opinions should help pin down the cause or causes, which can then be dealt with.

Pareto analysis. Frequently recurring problems may be several different problems, all linked and with many causes. In such circumstances, Pareto analysis can be useful in organising the data so that the most significant factors are clearly illustrated. This is based upon the 80–20 Pareto principle: that 80% of problems are caused by 20% of possible factors. To tackle a problem, therefore, concentrate on the troublemaking 20%. There are four key steps when initiating a Pareto analysis:

- ◪ Identify the overarching problem.
- ◪ Determine the factors causing it and how often they are to blame for the problem's occurrence.
- ◪ List the biggest factors contributing to the problem. Pareto

analysis is most useful when few factors are involved.
- Develop a solution targeting each factor individually.

This approach has the potential to eliminate the biggest causes of a problem, which often prevents it recurring or, at the very least, mitigates its effects. But it is less useful when a large number of factors are more or less equally responsible, as it is difficult and time consuming to analyse each one and pointless to prioritise the order in which they should be tackled. Pareto analysis works best when only damage control is possible. For example, all organisations get customer complaints, but the biggest reasons for customer dissatisfaction can be attended to, thus reducing the incidence of complaints. However, the more complicated the problem, the less likely it is that Pareto analysis will help to find a solution. For complex problems, creative problem solving is required.

Kepner-Tregoe analysis. Sometimes all that is needed is to determine what is wrong and why it is wrong, and then to fix it. This approach is at the heart of Kepner-Tregoe (KT) analysis and its emphasis on solid, rational analysis makes it suited to hard rather than soft management issues. For example, it is used to explain deviations from the norm, quality or process problems (often in manufacturing), and how to repair machines or systems and to identify potential problems.

KT analysis is simple, methodical and powerful. The first stage is to define the problem in detail by asking the following questions:

- What is the problem or deviation?
- Where does it occur?
- When does it (or did it) occur?
- How does it occur? Specifically, how often does it happen, and how old is the process when it first occurs?
- How big is the problem (how much is affected in real terms or as a proportion of the whole)?

The answers to these questions should allow you to define what the problem is, as well as what it is not. The next stage is to examine the differences between what should happen and what does happen, preparing a list of possible reasons for each difference and for the problem as a whole.

Techniques for creative problem solving

It is often said that in many organisations, too much attention is paid to norms, rules, procedures and precedents and not enough to creative thinking. However, many of the problems that organisations face today cannot be solved without a creative approach. Some of the most popular and effective approaches are described below.

Vertical and lateral thinking. Creativity can be divided into left-brain activities, those that are logical and analytical, and right-brain activities, those that are creative and integrative. A systematic approach to creativity is provided by Edward de Bono, who distinguished between vertical thinking, bounded by logic and linear thinking, and lateral thinking, which cuts across normal boundaries and processes. He claims that where traditional techniques are inadequate for solving problems, lateral thinking will generate new ideas and approaches that provide the answer. Lateral thinking combines ideas and concepts that have not previously been brought together. It removes assumptions, typically by asking "What if?" questions.

A questioning approach. Questioning is a useful starting point for creative problem solving. Challenging the way that things are can lead to alternatives being generated. Although questioning alone may not provide breakthrough thinking, it is often an essential first step in breaking traditional thinking. In particular, it can help to question established logic, asking "Why?" as well as "Why not?". Questioning the limits of existing processes, systems or technology can also stimulate creativity. Identifying false assumptions is another valuable step.

Accepting that good ideas come from anywhere. Ideas are no respecters of status or salary. It may be true that in certain industries senior people have the best ideas, and this is probably a reflection of their experience or confidence. However, excellent ideas can be found in unexpected places: junior members of staff, competitors, other industries or historical legend.

Maintaining momentum and avoiding drift. For the process of innovation to succeed, it is necessary to avoid drift and the dissipation of ideas. This can be achieved by pursuing a rigorous, focused approach and by setting tight deadlines. It can help to focus on issues such as customer needs and preferences, the strategic aims of the organisation, team and individual objectives, vision statements and goals that guide activities and progress, and information about competitors and other industries.

Removing constraints. Embracing radical change and re-engineering can help to foster innovation. Experience is valuable, but it is not everything. Something may never have been tried before, but this does not mean that it can never succeed. Another way to remove constraints is to make further use of the resources that are available, notably data, IT and the knowledge and experience of others. Moreover, motivation is important in driving innovation, and this means rewarding innovators.

Ensuring innovations are realistic. Whenever it is feasible, innovative proposals should be tested against practical realities. Those who generate ideas are not necessarily the best ones to check the practical implications, though in some cases they may be the only ones who can do this.

Planning the implementation of new ideas. New ideas often fail because of poor planning or execution, or because of a lack of communication and co-operation between the innovator and the implementer in making sure the vision is fulfilled but adapted as necessary according to practical and commercial considerations. Patient, critical analysis is more important in planning implementation of new ideas than it is for the initial process of innovation.

Brainstorming. One of the most popular methods of generating answers to problems is brainstorming, whereby those involved in the process come up with many solutions to a problem. Most will be inappropriate, but from the ideas generated it is hoped that a creative and effective solution will emerge. Brainstorming is a process in which a group employs all of its creative talent. However, it is only through the adoption of several important principles that it is likely to work.

- Quantity matters. Generate as many ideas as possible. Quality is secondary to the quantity of ideas. The quality of each idea can be assessed later.
- Suspend judgment. Prevent criticism or evaluation until as many ideas as possible have been produced, so that participants feel free to contribute without fear that their ideas will be torpedoed by others.
- Freewheel. Encourage every idea, even ones that may seem wild

and silly. The ideas that at first seem outlandish may be the ones of greatest brilliance.
- ◪ Cross-fertilise. Allow participants to build on each other's ideas in order to spawn new solutions that represent their collective thinking. This is how brainstorming becomes truly productive.
- ◪ Don't rush to judgment. Allow time between the generation of ideas and the evaluation process. A methodical process of elimination should be used to select the optimal solution. Set the criteria on which to rate the ideas generated. This helps to whittle down the ideas to a few promising solutions, of which one should be labelled frontrunner and the others kept as back-up alternatives.

Mind mapping. This is an approach that organises thoughts and ideas into a clear form, from which patterns and new approaches emerge or crystallise. Mind maps help to clarify issues, as well as to share and communicate ideas. A starting point is to list the pros and cons of each idea. Grouping issues into specific categories can also be useful. A popular example of this is SWOT analysis, which identifies internal strengths and weaknesses, and external opportunities and threats. Lastly, displaying ideas in diagrammatic form can highlight relationships between ideas.

Heuristics. A heuristic system uses experience to guide future plans and decisions. It is characterised by flexibility and tentativeness rather than forcefulness or certainty, with decisions adjusted as events develop, guided by a specific set of values. Thus heuristic methods work best in situations where structured or systematic decision-making methods cannot be applied, perhaps because the situation is new. Heuristics are relevant to the world of business: core principles (such as meeting customer needs or being an effective leader) combined with experience can be applied quickly and flexibly to effect a solution.

Implementing solutions
Before implementing any solution, other questions should be considered.

Is there a problem at all and does it need a solution? People and organisations rush into changes, often assuming that some action is necessary because something has occurred or may occur. Even if it has, it can sometimes be easier and less costly to ride out its effects.

Who is the best person to act? Important issues relating to shareholders or personnel are clearly the responsibility of senior managers. Many issues are cross-functional, which can complicate jurisdiction; and many are simply too complex to be addressed by one person alone. In any event, it is often useful to discuss situations with senior colleagues who are able to provide a different perspective or additional experience, even if their authority is not required.

Who should be involved? Identify in advance people whose help is essential and those who can be called upon should the need arise, and enlist their support. If implementation means a significant organisational change, then as well as those who lead the process there need to be influencers who can help to gain support and commitment. Any solution will rely on the skills and commitment of people.

What is the best way to plan, test and implement the solution? Planning is essential to ensure successful implementation. So is monitoring the implementation process, changing methods where necessary while still keeping the final goal clearly in mind. Contingency planning is valuable in overcoming any difficulties that may arise.

Developing problem-solving techniques
Problem-solving skills and processes, designed to prevent or overcome difficulties, should be improved during stable periods. If techniques have to be developed in the middle of a problem, then the process will become complex, distracted and overly experimental, making it harder to succeed. It is essential that solutions are practical and attainable within the organisation's resources, otherwise they are unlikely to work and may lead to additional problems.

International business decisions
Why do businesses expand internationally? The answer may be simple: to exploit markets and the economies of scale that come with expansion. But expanding into new geographical markets successfully is not simple to do.

Reasons for international expansion
Consider this question from the chairman of one of the largest industrial groups in the Asia-Pacific region:

> *How can our group of 20 diversified companies provide flexibility for each operating company to grow and innovate and, at the same time, reduce administrative overheads and employ information technology effectively across the group?*

And this, from the president of the largest division of one of the world's leading elevator companies:

> *Our business focuses on providing local services to customers in 22 countries. Will our biggest foreign competitor enter our region with a business infrastructure that relies on 22 country operations? No way!*

The reason for international expansion is generally to pursue an opportunity for growth; it may also be because existing markets are saturated. But business history is full of examples of companies whose international ventures do not succeed as intended. UK retailer Marks & Spencer, for example, believed it could broaden its revenue base by expanding internationally, only to find that it didn't work. It has since closed or sold most of its foreign operations and focused on its core UK market.

Some firms expand abroad because their market as a whole is an international one, as it is for such industries as entertainment, publishing, pharmaceuticals and telecoms. Or it may be because the domestic market is too small, as it is for such industries as aerospace, shipbuilding and automotive manufacturing.

However, decisions to expand internationally are probably driven by less rational factors or by conjecture. International expansion may result from a desire to exploit a much larger market, which can then be justified with spurious interpretations of data. There is prima facie evidence of this from two sources. The first is the dotcom explosion that occurred during the 1990s, when many entrepreneurs and their backers believed that a global market existed for whatever was being sold. The key was simply to get online, drive traffic to the site and gain market share. The internet came to be seen as a fast track to securing a strong global position. The second is the keenness of firms to expand into China during the 1980s and 1990s. Many saw China as the most promising market in the world, and many have so far been sorely disappointed. Pursuing foreign markets is invariably much more complex than it may appear at first sight. It can also be largely untried.

It has to be said that hubris may also play a part. If the opportunity exists for overseas expansion, a firm's leaders may feel obliged to expand there. Not to do so may be a tacit admission of failure. Or an ambitious CEO may just be bored with the current business and want a new challenge.

Succeeding with international decisions

Strategic decisions about international expansion must take into account all kinds of things, including market entry, product development and production sales and service, marketing and distribution. Substantial costs and risk may be involved, and the following steps should be taken.

Defining objectives. The first priority is to be clear about what your international strategy can and cannot achieve. There should also be clearly defined success criteria: many firms stage the implementation of their international expansion, only committing additional resources when initial objectives have been achieved. A helpful question to ask might be: "What level of achievement would be acceptable to the business, regardless of how the market is perceived?" Other questions include the following:

- How does the international strategy help to achieve the overall aims of the organisation?
- What are the priorities (cross-selling or improving service for existing customers, attracting new clients, attacking current or potential competitors, reducing costs, gaining information and experience, or something else)?
- What are the options? For example, should the firm set up an overseas office or subsidiary, or would acquisition, a joint venture, franchising or licensing be better approaches?
- Where are the potential pitfalls and how will the risk be managed?
- Does the organisational structure need to be altered to take full advantage of the international operations? If so, how?

Understanding the market. Many firms think that they understand a foreign market when they do not. There are a number of examples of British firms (Marks & Spencer and EMAP are two) going into the United States and getting it badly wrong. You need to understand how progress is made, how things are done and what the principal issues, including cultural ones, are. How will the organisation be perceived? Is everyone involved prepared for doing business in an environment that may be different? As discussed in Chapter 7, cultural issues are particularly significant in cross-border mergers or acquisitions. One lesson from successful mergers is that it is often best to recognise cultural differences, show flexibility and compromise, and work hard at developing a unitary set of values. Common systems and integrated objectives can help achieve this.

Assessing organisational issues. There are many areas where an overseas expansion can run into difficulty. Are employees prepared, motivated, trained and equipped to do business internationally? What practical difficulties and barriers to expansion are there in the short and medium term? Another area requiring consideration is the communication of the decision. How will existing customers, employees and shareholders react to the decision to expand overseas? Are there opportunities to raise the profile of the organisation and facilitate its entry into the new market? To better understand such organisational issues, it makes sense to use external advisers with experience of the market. Government agencies and trade associations can also provide help and so, too, can other, non-competing businesses. Local personnel with expertise in the market can be recruited to advise on the best way of succeeding in a new market.

Establishing operations abroad. Analysing the available options will highlight the best approach and inform the way in which it is executed. A strategy to expand internationally requires a champion, someone with dynamism and commitment, and ideally with local expertise or expertise in setting up a similar expansion elsewhere. Such a champion must be flexible enough to make adjustments as necessary to make the new strategy succeed, and must have (or have a subordinate who has) good project management skills in order to provide focus and prioritise actions and aims.

Structuring international operations. It can be unproductive and a waste of resources to make a new international firm fit existing systems and procedures. But core management issues such as communications, structure and leadership are best resolved early. Managers must ensure that information and expertise flow freely throughout the organisation. In particular, best-practice information should be widely disseminated and available for everyone in the organisation.

Deciding the degree of autonomy given to international business units is fundamental. Reporting structures, responsibilities and authority levels need to be clear. An organisation benefits from being integrated and cohesive and should be fair and consistent in its practices and with its employees. Local factors should be taken into account, but an organisation should be true to its values. Co-ordination and control are important; if left to drift, international operations become disconnected from the rest of the organisation, even in conflict with it.

Leading and motivating people, setting direction and making decisions are all made more difficult across borders. Empowerment often provides a solution, enabling people to work within clearly defined areas of responsibility. Mentoring schemes can provide individuals with support and coaching, helping to integrate international business units into the organisation as a whole.

Ensuring stability and efficiency. Multinational companies will want to reduce costs and maximise resources within a single, integrated structure. Things to consider when determining the best structure include:

- Political, economic and other factors affecting stability. If the operating environment is unstable, then the best solution may be to provide direct support.
- Resources: human, financial and so on.
- The purpose, size and complexity of the operation. Generally, the more sophisticated and complex the organisation, the more autonomy is required. But good communications between local operations and overseas headquarters are always important.

Communicating. When building an international business, all those with a stake in the company, especially shareholders, providers of finance and employees, should be informed of what is happening, what the advantages are and what it means for them. Without an explanation, people often fear the worst. Without a convincing explanation, they worry that the management has not thought things through and may be making a strategic error.

Connected business units: Hewlett-Packard's IT advantage

Between 1987 and 1997, Hewlett-Packard significantly reduced the cost structure of its global business while increasing revenue from $5 billion to $40 billion and maintaining a headcount of around 100,000 people. Sales, general and administrative expenses fell from 28% of turnover to 17%.

The company did this by being responsive to, and supportive of, its business units around the world. Global networks and an IT infrastructure geared to effective information sharing, promoting best practice and allowing a rapid response to implementing vital changes considerably strengthened Hewlett-Packard's position. For example, the company bills all IT costs (including employees' e-mails) to business-unit managers to encourage awareness of costs. Furthermore, the culture of information-sharing across business units encourages the exchange of best-practice expertise and knowledge between business units.

A global IT infrastructure allows business units to concentrate on value-creation and promoting growth. Combining business flexibility with IT standardisation helps greatly when coping with rapid international industry change.

Financial issues

The commercial issues associated with any major new undertaking include:

- Transfer pricing. The prices at which an organisation transfers goods between subsidiaries in different countries will affect local profitability and may have tax implications.
- Exchange rate volatility. Changes in the value of currencies complicate cross-border business and can affect profitability. For firms operating within the euro zone, reducing this uncertainty is seen as a benefit of the single European currency. Firms can, of course, hedge their currency risks by buying and selling currencies forward, but the fewer currencies you have to work with the simpler is the administration.
- Taxation and accounting differences, and legal and other local requirements. These will affect the way the business should be set up and managed.

Key questions

- Understanding people's motivation and patterns of behaviour is fundamental for everyone involved in strategic decision-making. Are people motivated?
- A vital element in empowering people is ensuring that they understand and accept where the boundaries of their authority lie. Is this clear for everyone in the organisation, and are these boundaries in the right place?
- Are safeguards in place with regard to the execution of financial, legal and regulatory decisions?
- Are the following implications of reversal theory understood and used to guide decision-making?
  - The goal is not necessarily the most important thing – sometimes it is the means that drives decisions.
  - A decision may require conformity, or it may require a rebellious approach.
  - The degree of control required for a decision to be effective can vary.
  - Relationships matter when making decisions.
- Are operational decisions effectively executed? How good is the organisation at delivering the details?
- Are people in the organisation able to question established practice? Is the organisation sufficiently creative and supportive, or could this be improved?
- Do people in the organisation work together to share ideas and solve problems, or does work need to be done to break down barriers and parochialism?

Mastering international decisions can enhance every aspect of the organisation, exposing people to new ideas and approaches as well as gaining the commercial advantages of diversity. The risks are great but so too are the potential benefits. Consider the following issues before starting or reviewing international activities:

- How well defined is the overall strategy for international growth?
- What is the best approach (for example, joint venture, acquisition, licensing or some other commercial option), and have all possible options been considered?
- What factors are driving growth internationally, internally (within the organisation) and externally?

- What are the financial implications of this approach? Who is responsible for managing costs and risks, and how are these being monitored?
- What is the single most important goal and how will this be achieved? Where is the single greatest risk and how is this being approached?
- Every situation is different: what makes this one distinctive and why?
- How will this strategy affect other aspects of the business and in particular key stakeholders (notably customers, employees, suppliers, shareholders)?
- What level of performance would be satisfactory, leading to further investment? What are the success criteria, and are they really realistic?
- Who is responsible for leading the international business?
- What is the medium- to long-term plan that will ensure that the firm's success can be sustained?
- What activities are involved? Is there a detailed plan, and is there an understanding of the complexities of this decision?
- Is there a need to restructure systems, such as communications and information management, to ensure that the organisation is fully integrated?
- Has the decision been communicated? Are people informed and mobilised to succeed?

6 Scenario thinking

In establishing a strategic direction and a set of priorities that will guide decision-makers, few techniques are as powerful as scenario thinking (also known as scenario planning). Scenarios are perspectives on potential events and their consequences, providing a context in which managers can make decisions. By contemplating a range of possible futures, decisions are better informed, and a strategy based on this deeper insight is more likely to succeed.

Scenarios help managers tackle risk, uncertainty and complexity, enabling better strategy development. Scenario planning enables organisations to rehearse the future, to walk the battlefield before battle commences so that they are better prepared. As Philip Watts, chairman of Royal Dutch/Shell Group, says:

> Scenarios are not predictions. Rather they are a way of challenging our assumptions. They are a tool for focusing on critical uncertainties – the unexpected discontinuities or unknown possibilities which could transform our business environment.

In his book *Competitive Advantage*, Michael Porter defines a scenario as "an internally consistent view of what the future might turn out to be – not a forecast, but one possible future outcome".[1]

Scenario thinking has been used by the military for centuries and by organisations such as Shell since the 1960s. According to Kees van der Heijden:

> Scenario planning is neither an episodic activity nor a new technique: it is a way of thinking that works best when it permeates the entire organisation, affecting decisions at all levels. However, unlike most popular management initiatives, it does not require major investment in resources or restructuring, simply a commitment for people to take time away from their routine activities to come together to reflect and learn.[2]

Scenarios may not predict the future, but they do illuminate the causes of change – which helps managers to take greater control when market conditions shift. An organisation's future success will depend much on how managers react to what they do not know. As Mark Twain put it:

> The important thing is not how much we don't know, as how wrong we are in what we think we do know.

The benefits of scenario planning

Understanding the present. Scenario planning helps provide a better understanding of how different factors affecting a business effect each other. It can reveal linkages between apparently unrelated factors and, most importantly, it can provide greater insight into the forces shaping the future, delivering real competitive advantage. Watts believes that "there are two things we can say for certain about that future. It will be different – and it will surprise".

Overcoming complacency. Scenarios should be designed to challenge established views, to overcome business-as-usual complacency and to enable both established formulas and new ideas to be tested. Seeing reality from different perspectives mitigates the pitfalls of groupthink, fragmentation, procrastination, hindsight bias, shifting responsibility and bolstering commitment to failing strategies (see Chapter 3). As Ged Davis, vice-president, global business environment, at Shell says:

> Much forecasting consists of little more than optimistic or pessimistic views of developments from a present position. This "tyranny of the present" arises from the fact that we are strongly influenced by those around us.

Promoting action and ownership of the strategy process. Scenario planning helps break the constraints on traditional strategic practices, as it enables those involved to discuss the complexity and ambiguity of their perspectives in a wide context. Davis highlights this:

> Scenarios attempt to look beyond our more limited mindsets, recognising that possibilities are influenced by a wide range of people and that many views of the world are different from our own.

Stimulating creativity and innovation. Scenarios encourage the opening of minds to new possibilities and the excitement of thinking about how they may be realised. The process leads to a positive attitude that actively seeks the desired outcome.

Promoting learning. Scenarios help people to understand their environment, consider the future, share knowledge and evaluate strategic options. Information is better evaluated and integrated in the scenario planning process, which enables those involved in it to recognise and react to emerging circumstances. Watts speaks for many CEOs when he says:

> *None of us needs reminding today how unexpected events –*
> *beyond imagination – can set the world on a new path ... Our*
> *aim is to be prepared for a wider range of eventualities –*
> *ideally, to be able to interpret as normal human affairs what*
> *others see as crises.*

Creating a shared view. Scenario planning works because it looks beyond current assignments, facts and forecasts. It allows discussions to be more uninhibited and it creates the conditions for a genuinely effective shared sense of purpose to evolve. This should mean that the strategic decisions reached through scenario planning have widespread support.

Saving billions with scenarios: Pierre Wack and Shell

One of the first users of scenarios in business in the 1960s was Shell. The process was largely driven by Pierre Wack, head of group planning, whose view was that:

> *Scenarios help us to understand today better by imagining tomorrow,*
> *increasing the breadth of vision and enabling us to spot change earlier ...*
> *Effective future thinking brings a reduction in the level of crisis*
> *management and improves management capability, particularly change*
> *management.*

The company created a unit, managed by Wack, to overcome problems of cash-flow management and to forecast future cash requirements. When traditional techniques for forecasting cash flow ran into problems, Wack's diagnosis was that they were trying to apply statistical techniques to variables that were fundamentally unpredictable. He realised that fundamental uncertainties had be distinguished from what could be predicted. So the team started to discuss what was predictable, in this case the future of the global oil price and issues of supply and demand. Since global demand for oil had grown consistently by 6–8 % per annum since 1945, demand was initially assumed to be a predetermined factor. This led the team to focus on supply. Engineers assured the group that availability would not be a technical problem, so most people at Shell assumed that traditional price trends would continue.

Wack was not satisfied. He wanted to know if there were other factors in supply, besides technical availability, that might be more uncertain. By listing stakeholders, the team quickly identified another factor: governments in oil-producing countries. Wack posed the questions: would these governments be happy to continue to increase production year on year, and would this be in their interest? Through role-play, the team analysed the policy options available. It became apparent that many oil-producing countries did not need an increase in income and that the overwhelming logic for them was to reduce supply, increase prices and conserve their reserves.

When Wack outlined this to his superiors, he was told that there was a lack of unity among oil-producing countries and that the oil companies were in practice able to control supply. His response was to sharpen the scenario to include growth in demand and the increasing realisation by OPEC countries of the strength of their position if they acted in concert. As Wack commented:

> Participating in the scenario-building process improves a management team's ability to manage uncertainty and risk. Risky decisions become more transparent and key threats and opportunities are identified.

Then the scenario became reality. The 1973 Israeli–Arab war had a dramatic impact, limiting the supply of oil. As a result, prices rose fivefold. Fortunately for Shell, Wack's work had encouraged the company to be prepared for such a change, and when it happened, Shell was streets ahead of its competitors, enabling it to climb from seventh to second place in the oil firm's profitability league table.

Scenarios remain a vital part of Shell's approach because as Philip Watts, the chairman, points out:

> Using scenarios helps us understand the dynamics of the business environment, recognise new opportunities, assess strategic options and take long-term decisions.

For Shell, scenario thinking is an essential strategic tool. Ged Davis explains:

> It is quite normal in the energy and resources industries ... to be dealing
> with projects that have very long lead times. A typical large-scale gas
> project might require an investment of $10 billion, take six years from the
> decision to invest to come on stream, and have a life of at least 20 years.
> Thus the review of such a project requires thinking of at least 25 years.

Shell's experience demonstrates that scenarios provide an effective mechanism for assessing existing strategies and for developing and assessing options. The scenario planning process helps underpin and develop the strengths of an organisation and makes it more sensitive to the early-warning signs of trouble ahead.

Using scenario thinking

The scenario thinking process is not one of linear implementation, providing a single snapshot; its effectiveness lies in stimulating decisions, what Van der Heijden calls the strategic conversation.[3] This is the continuous process of planning, analysing the environment, generating and testing scenarios, developing options, selecting, refining and implementing: a process that is itself refined with further environmental analysis. Steps in using the scenario process include:

- Planning and structuring the scenario process
- Exploring the scenario context
- Developing the scenarios
- Analysing the scenarios
- Using the scenarios

Planning and structuring the scenario process

The first stage is to identify gaps in organisational knowledge that relate specifically to business challenges whose impact on the organisation is uncertain. The next step is to create a team to plan and structure the process. The team should probably come from outside the organisation, and its members should be noted for their creative thinking and ability to challenge conventional ideas. An external team is better placed to provide objective support, free from internal agendas or tensions. In discussion with the team, then decide on the duration of the project; ten weeks is considered appropriate for a big project.

Exploring the scenario context

A few employees should be chosen to participate in the workshop team that will explore possible scenarios. They should be interviewed separately by the external team to identify their views, which should then be assessed and explored by the whole team. Questions should focus on vital issues – such as sources of customer value, the current success formula and future challenges – and identify how each individual views the past, present and future aspects of each.

According to George Cairns, a professor at the University of Strathclyde Graduate School of Business:

> The interview statements should be collated and analysed in an interview report, structured around the recurring concepts and key themes. This now sets the agenda for the first workshop and should be sent to all participants. It is also valuable to identify the critical uncertainties and issues, as perceived by the participants, as a starting point for the workshop.

Developing the scenarios

The workshop should identify the forces that will have an impact over an agreed period. Two possible opposite outcomes should be agreed and the forces that could lead to each of them should be listed. This will help show how these forces link together. Next decide whether these forces will have a low or high impact and a low or high probability. This information should be stored on a 2×2 matrix.

With two opposite outcomes and the driving forces clearly presented, the team can then develop the likely "histories", or scenarios, that led to each outcome. These histories of the future can then be expanded through discussion of the forces behind the changes. The aim is not to develop accurate predictions, but to understand what will shape the future and how different events interact and influence each other. All the time, discussions are focused on each scenario's impact on the organisation.

This part of the process opens up the thinking of the members of the team and makes them alert to signals that may suggest a particular direction for the organisation. The outcomes of different responses are "tested" in the safety of scenario planning, thus avoiding the risk of implementing a strategy for real.

Analysing the scenarios

The analysis stage examines the external issues and internal logic. What are the priorities and concerns of those outside the organisation also responsible for the main decisions in the scenario? Who are the other stakeholders? The internal logic involves asking who the key players are and whether they change. Would they really act and make decisions in the way described? Systems and process diagrams can help address these questions, as can discussions with other stakeholders.

At this point in the process, it is helpful to remember Shell's approach to scenarios, outlined by Watts:

> We don't aim to pinpoint future events – but to consider the
> forces which may push the future along different paths.

Using the scenarios

Working backwards from the future to the present, the team should formulate an action plan that can influence the organisation's thinking. Then it should identify the early signs of change so that when they occur they will be recognised and responded to quickly and effectively.

The process continues by identifying gaps in organisational knowledge. For Van der Heijden, the continuation of the strategic conversation and its integration into the routine thoughts of individuals reduces risk and promotes success:

> The participatory and creative process sensitises managers to
> the outside world. It helps individuals and teams learn to
> recognise the uncertainties in their operating environments, so
> that they can question their everyday assumptions, adjust their
> mental maps, and truly think outside the box in a cohesive
> fashion.

Scenarios are tools for examining possible futures. This gives them a clear advantage over techniques that may be based on a view of the past. In a rapidly changing and largely unpredictable environment, assessing possible futures is one of the best ways to promote responsiveness and directed policy. Understanding and preparing for the future are certainly possible through scenario planning. The financial value of scenarios compared with traditional approaches is highlighted by Watts:

Those that rely solely on forecasting in their thinking about the future can find the consequences very expensive.

Some key points to bear in mind are as follows:

- Scenario planning works best when it involves people at all levels of the organisation.
- Scenarios must be relevant.
- Critically assessing each scenario keeps the process focused, relevant and valuable.
- Don't try to predict the future; instead, try to understand the forces that will shape it.
- Encourage creative thinking, and do not allow existing biases to guide the process. Also ensure that the process is not overshadowed by operational pressures, as these can limit energy and creativity.
- Understand the insights, and relate them to the organisation's future.

Key questions

Before embarking on scenario planning, consider the following questions:

- Do the current strategic approaches typify traditional, business-as-usual thinking? Are you prepared to accept that a strategy is failing or is vulnerable?
- Is the organisation in touch with market developments and the needs of customers? Are you prepared to challenge your confidence in existing orthodoxy?
- Is any part of your organisational planning weak and lacking clear direction? Do you lack confidence in your ability to engage in strategic debate?
- In your decision-making process do you, routinely, always consider multiple options before deciding? Is the quality of your strategic thinking limited, narrow and uninspired?
- Is your organisation afraid of uncertainty, or does it enjoy thinking about it? Do people see it as a threat or as an opportunity? Is it recognised as a potential source of competitive advantage?

7 Strategies for growth

One of the most fundamental decisions for any organisation is to choose the most effective strategy for growth. It is tempting to believe that doing in the future what has been done in the past will lead to continued growth – "if it ain't broke, don't fix it" – but the past is no guarantee for the future. Continuing down the same path may lead to continuing success or it may lead off a cliff. If managers are to make the right decisions, therefore, a strategic direction and set of guiding priorities are needed together with an assessment of the most effective strategy for growth.

The different routes to growth fall broadly into five options:

- Organic growth
- Mergers and acquisitions
- Integration
- Diversification
- Specialisation

The characteristics of each are outlined below, but they are not mutually exclusive and can overlap. They are, however, limited by the resources available and all require a clear focus on objectives and a sustained level of commitment.

Organic growth

This is when a business grows from its own resources. Organic growth can happen because the market is growing or because a firm is doing increasingly better than its competitors or is going into new markets. Exploiting a product advantage can sustain organic growth; examples are a law firm with a star partner or a software firm with a unique programme. But there is only so much growth that one person or one product can generate and people eventually retire and products mature, so organic growth normally requires launching new products or product extensions, entering new markets or establishing wider distribution networks and sales agency agreements, or licensing or franchising.

Organic growth depends on a number of things outlined below.

Core competences and capabilities

Organic growth depends largely on what an organisation is good at and capable of. It is helped by identifying and exploiting synergies across different parts of an organisation's activities; by structuring the organisation to take advantage of "priority" opportunities; and by creating a culture that is able to spot opportunities when they arise and make the most of them.

Planning

Growth can be achieved quickly and unexpectedly, but for it to be sustained a co-ordinated plan of action is needed among business functions such as marketing, production, finance and human resources. Organic growth gives an organisation total control over the process of development and relies on the experience and expertise within the firm.

Time

Growing organically can be a slow process, as with acorns that become mighty oak trees. It requires patience, application and strong, focused leadership to keep the strategy on course and maintain support for it.

Cash

Cash is essential for organic growth, preferably cash generated from within the business being used to develop other parts, or cash provided as a loan or in return for an equity stake in the business. Cash is needed to pay for expansion and new developments, either by taking on new staff, buying in new resources (such as IT systems), developing and producing new products or undertaking marketing initiatives.

Mergers and acquisitions

The fastest route to growth is through an acquisition or merger. But more than half fail to add value and they are notoriously difficult to pull off successfully.

A hard drive: Hewlett-Packard's merger with Compaq

Hewlett-Packard's $21 billion takeover of Compaq in 2001 and 2002 was a bitterly fought battle. The champion of the bid, Carly Fiorina, HP's CEO, pitted herself against Walter Hewlett, who headed a counter charge of the powerful and influential of Silicon Valley. The battle was vigorous and acrimonious with Fiorina emerging the victor when shareholders voted in favour of the merger by 51.4% to 48.6%. On March 19th 2002, Fiorina declared the deal approved by "a slim but sufficient margin".

Even after the vote, which involved numerous recounts, Hewlett refused to concede defeat and brought an action against HP in a Texas court. Between the announcement of the deal in September 2001 and Fiorina's statement on March 19th 2002, HP's stock price had fallen by 17% and Compaq's had plummeted by 27%; in contrast, IBM's shares rose 12%.

This case highlights two different views about mergers. One is that mergers between titans will result in an even larger titan, too cumbersome to operate flexibly and efficiently, which in many industries (and certainly for technology-based businesses) is vital. In this view, a merger results in:

- more bureaucracy;
- diminishing returns negating the benefits of increases in size and capacity for production;
- diseconomies of scale, swallowing huge quantities of capital and causing organisational lethargy;
- a lumbering giant that will be outpaced and outsmarted by smaller rivals.

The second, more optimistic, view is that mergers result in organisations that:

- achieve economies of scale and are more efficient;
- are stable and broadly based;
- have the intellectual capital and management infrastructure that will allow them to deal effectively with market change.

These types of organisations, the argument goes, are better for both society and stakeholders. They most closely resemble Herculean giants, gods among markets, operating with faultless precision, in-depth experience and fluid efficiency to maximise revenue. Markets consisting of such organisations, according to Joseph Schumpeter, an economist, are better for all parties in society as there is an absence of factionalism. This works best in industries where there are only a few main competitors.

Both views are valid. Assessing which is most applicable to the merger between HP and Compaq is an interesting and illuminating exercise. When the merger was announced in September 2001, HP's management said:

> We recognise that integrating two cultures – each with its own distinct heritage – is a challenge. But the success of the combined company depends upon building a strong common culture.

Arguments for the merger

Fiorina staked her career on the merger. Brought in three years earlier from Lucent Technologies to revive HP, which was seen as excessively bureaucratic, Fiorina believed that the merger would diversify both HP and Compaq, broadening their reach into different markets. This would take place against a background of lethargic growth in the technology sector, which in turn would drive industry consolidation. The undeniable logic says that in tough economic conditions the successful firm must become leaner, with lower fixed costs, and more aggressive, able to win the dwindling numbers of potential customers. She believed that the combined company would be a formidable force benefiting from:

- increased capital assets, enabling economies of scale;
- opportunities to gain a hold or a share of a new market (whether identified by territory or product);
- the opportunity to restructure and refocus the company;
- additional channels to control the supply of goods and the supply to customers (as with mergers between companies in different sections of the supply chain);
- diminished competition, as a result of two principal firms in a market merging to increase their market share.

Arguments against the merger

There are many problems to overcome in any merger. As the HP management statement of September 2001 accepted, without "a strong common culture" a merger is doomed to failure. Moreover, without sufficient planning pre- and post-merger it is likely to be fruitless, benefiting only competitors, and no more than a short-term measure. The long-term consequences can be significant, eroding shareholder value and destroying stakeholders' interests.

Hewlett, son of one of the company's founders and a significant shareholder, argued that the merger would dilute HP's hugely successful printing operation with a far lower margin PC business. Furthermore, there was dissent and dissatisfaction among staff, shareholders and customers.

CBIS, an HP shareholder, voted against the merger, explaining in a press release:

> *CEO Carleton S Fiorina has received compensation packages over the last several years of $30–90m per year, far in excess of what our participants consider reasonable, and particularly unacceptable in light of underperformance of the company during the same period.*

CBIS also said that the premium being paid for Compaq was excessive given the risk involved, and that poor corporate governance policies caused entrenched management attitudes and reduced incentives for managers to work in the interest of shareholders.

In 1989, HP led the market for the RISC workstation, competing strongly with Apollo and Sun Microsystems. According to Hewlett, when HP acquired Apollo it executed the merger poorly, failing to leverage its new assets. This meant that HP failed to gain market share and the diminished level of competition was advantageous to Sun Microsystems, which went on to dominate the market.

The verdict

Mergers are easy to contemplate and difficult to execute. A recent study by Booz, Allen and Hamilton, a management consultancy, highlighted that of all American companies that carried out mergers between 1997 and 1998, about two-thirds cited bad planning and execution as the reasons for the mergers failing to fully realise their supposed potential.

HP has taken some measures considered to be best practice when merging, and it may be the case that the opposition led by Hewlett, together with the shareholders' narrow mandate, resulted in a more rigorous approach. The establishment of a 600-strong integration office to plan and co-ordinate the merger allowed many changes to be executed without a hitch, while also establishing damage control over what was always going to be a messy process. The post-merger company has increased the competitive pressure on IBM and Dell in a difficult period of low economic growth.

Some mergers are defensive, initiated because the companies involved are under threat: McDonnell Douglas merged with Boeing because their main customer, the Pentagon, slashed expenditure by half. Mergers can also result from intensified globalisation: Chrysler merged with Daimler-Benz because they were warned about their ability to prosper in a global business environment. The threat may arise from a single foe: Bayerische Vereinsbank merged with Bavarian rival Hypobank to avoid being taken over by their greater rival Deutsche Bank. Such mergers are rarely positive. Mergers that are more likely to work are those with clear advantages in mind, rather than those aiming to minimise disadvantages.

The jury is still out on whether the merger between HP and Compaq will prove to have been a smart move. However, despite the numerous problems associated with the merger, there is something impressive about its background and execution. It was aggressive, designed by companies struggling in their markets against formidable competitors. It also has positive elements and a detailed plan for success. The merger of AOL and Time Warner succeeded initially because it was an offensive move. When planning a merger, this is a good premise from which to launch. Some companies merge so that they can hide their losses, some to gain capital assets, some to gain intangible assets and intellectual property, and some to reduce competition; but successful companies are always clear about advantages and do not ignore dissent among stakeholders.

The real test of success is perhaps the extent to which a merger provides a platform for future development. The thorough, resilient and bold tactics practised by Fiorina give promise to the HP and Compaq merger. However, this will be meaningless if the advantages are not fully realised, or if dissent spirals out of control. The merger highlights the principle that your enemies should be contained and competition sustained, or else a hard drive may turn floppy.

Succeeding with M&A decisions

Mergers and acquisitions (M&As) are increasingly important for many firms; this applies especially to medium and large undertakings and those operating in more than one market. In particular, liberalisation of trade and globalisation of business and financial markets have boosted activity in them. In 2001, merger activity reached a peak and then dropped dramatically as firms reacted to economic uncertainties and wild stockmarket fluctuations. Such cautious conservatism won't last: an M&A is such a potentially powerful route to growth and competitive advantage that as soon as economic confidence returns, so will M&A mania. Even before then, plucky entrepreneurs and bold shareholders may see opportunities to pick up a bargain, such as a sound business that may have encountered short-term difficulties.

However, problems are common following business mergers, with 48% of merged companies underperforming in their industry after three years, according to a 1997 report by Mercer Management Consulting. An enquiry conducted and published in the *Harvard Business Review* (November 1997) highlighted this point:

> *Fewer than 50% of mergers ever reach anywhere near the economic or strategic destination that was envisioned for them. In fact, in many cases the mergers fail because the new company's managers underestimated, ignored, or mishandled the integration tasks.*

Anecdotal evidence from business analysts and commentators suggests that although this information is now some years old, it still holds true. Mergers are no more a guarantee of growth and prosperity today than they ever were.

Decisions on whether to merge with or acquire a business are complex and usually involve a high degree of risk. If the decision to merge is well judged and the implementation of the merger is well executed, it can result in large-scale, rapid growth. However, if you make a bad decision or implement it badly, it can have a hugely damaging effect on business resources and profits.

Three stages of the merger or acquisition process
Planning and preparation
Decision 1: decide your strategy. The first step in developing a strategy includes a top-down strategic vision based on the advantages of acquisition versus other approaches, such as joint ventures or organic growth. Clear understanding of the market sector in general and the strengths and weaknesses of all the players involved in particular will also help to inform the strategy.

This vision determines how the business approaches the deal: what is to be gained, likely targets or partners and the rationale for the deal. Coupled with this is the bottom-up approach, where lower-level managers or, in the case of a group, senior managers at subsidiary level are involved in the strategic process as they can highlight potential pitfalls as well as more positive future developments that may be overlooked. They may also provide useful market information, such as a target's strengths and weaknesses or specific opportunities.

Decision 2: identify and select targets. When seeking a suitable acquisition or merger target, include the following:

- A target specification: attributes that are either essential or desirable for a target company to possess.
- The opportunities available in the sector and a list of potential candidates, ranked in priority order.
- What each target offers and how it will fit, in theory and in practice, with the business.
- Who to approach, how and when.

Decision 3: decide specific objectives and understand how issues affect them. Be clear about the deal's objectives, which may include gaining access to intellectual property assets or new markets, providing synergies with existing activities, increasing capacity, or simply removing a competitor.

Assessing the current and potential value of the target business means taking into account factors such as tangible and intangible assets, notably property and intellectual property, and the expertise of its personnel and the likelihood that they will remain. Investigate the target business's management expertise and organisational culture: the way that the business is run and decisions are made, as well as its culture and values. Then assess what benefits these would bring and what difficulties they may cause in the integration process.

Assess what you might have to pay in order to win support from the target company's (and your firm's) shareholders and other interested parties. Work out who else's support you need: key managers, the media, stockmarket analysts or whatever. All this affects the ease with which the company can be acquired as well as the depth of long-term support and cash that may be available for future developments, such as a process of costly restructuring.

Due diligence

Due diligence is the process of investigating a target company in detail. The purpose and value of due diligence are not only commercial, for instance ensuring that the business is fully understood and that the acquisition proceeds successfully; it is also to provide a financial and legal audit. Due diligence involves examining the target's accounts, contracts and all other commercial aspects. It provides a basis for identifying and avoiding risks, ensuring accurate valuation and preparing for post-acquisition integration, and, in particular, understanding the many people issues that invariably determine the ease and success of the merger.

For these reasons due diligence is often conducted in parallel with contract negotiations, although some advisers recommend that it follows negotiation and is completed as the last stage before the deal is executed.

Decision 4: price and structure the deal. The issue of price is paramount. It will depend on whether it is a buyer's or a seller's market, and it is important to make a judgment about the seller's bottom line. A decision must also be made on the buyer's top line, which should take into account the additional costs on top of the purchase price: for example, fees paid to legal and any other advisers; the cost of raising capital and financing the acquisition; tax considerations; integration costs to realise the full potential of the acquisition; and legal completion costs.

Once due diligence has been completed and any surprises it has uncovered have been taken into account, contracts can be drawn up.

Decision 5: negotiate the deal. Negotiations often run alongside due diligence, but there will be a final stage when things like warranties and indemnities, designed to protect the acquirer against surprises not revealed by the due diligence process, are agreed.

Post-acquisition planning and integration
Whatever precedes this stage can still be rendered worthless if the ultimate purpose of the deal – the successful integration of the target – is not achieved. An effective post-acquisition strategy is therefore a vital component of a successful acquisition, and post-acquisition planning needs to start before the deal is finalised.

Decision 6: plan early to realise the benefits of the deal. Post-acquisition integration decisions should take into account:

- the overall strategy of the business;
- the culture and management styles of the two organisations;
- issues of presentation, communication and understanding;
- customer-focused market issues – it may be a grand plan, but how will customers, current and potential, react? Can this be turned to the acquirer's advantage?
- people management issues, in particular motivation, empowerment and innovation;

management procedures and systems, especially for IT and finance; the need to inform shareholders.

One of the most intriguing mergers of recent years was the deal between Germany's Daimler-Benz and America's Chrysler Corporation. It was intriguing for many reasons, not least because initially it was far from clear whether it was a merger between approximate equals or an acquisition by the larger Daimler. It became clear it was in effect the latter. It provides a valuable case study of the perils of structuring a massive corporate deal.

DaimlerChrysler: revenues, profits and employment, 1997

	Daimler-Benz	Chrysler Corporation	DaimlerChrysler
Revenues ($m)	68,917	61,147	130,064
Operating profit ($m)	2,404	4,723	7,127
Employees (no.)	300,168	121,000	421,168

Source: Daimler and Chrysler published accounts.

A long road to prosperity: Daimler's merger with Chrysler

On May 7th 1998 two of the world's leading car manufacturers, Daimler-Benz and Chrysler Corporation, announced the largest industrial merger in history. The new company, DaimlerChrysler, was the world's fifth-largest carmaker with revenues of $130 billion, an operating profit of $7 billion and a workforce of more than 420,000 (see table).

Chrysler and Daimler-Benz were strong in two different markets: North America and western Europe respectively. The merged company, DaimlerChrysler, was designed to force its way into new markets, particularly in Asia but also in South America and eastern Europe. New markets require new products that are tailored to their needs, and the combined forces of these motoring giants were seen as having the capability to innovate effectively. In July 2002, against a backdrop of continuing economic uncertainty and turbulence on the world's stockmarkets, DaimlerChrysler announced higher than expected profits compared with the previous dismal year, signalling to the world that the merger had at last started delivering some of the long awaited benefits. However, the early years of the merged business were difficult and painful, and it is still far from certain whether one set of good results will translate into long-term success.

The merger came at the right time for Chrysler, according to Susan Jacobs of Jacobs & Associates:

> The US market is saturated, and the company's only avenue for growth is overseas. Chrysler has only 1% market share in Europe.

Jacobs also believed that Chrysler's brands – Jeep, Dodge and Plymouth – could break into markets that were closed to Mercedes. C. Fred Bergsten, director of the Institute for International Economics in Washington DC, saw the merger as a "win-win proposition", believing it would improve the efficiency of the two companies. Instead of one partner being "rescued" by the merger, the DaimlerChrysler union was seen as a merger of equals, prompted not by necessity but by opportunity, at least superficially. Daimler-Benz was known for its engineering skill and Chrysler was known for innovation, speed in product development and bold marketing. Chrysler and Daimler-Benz products were complementary with little overlap. Moreover, potential growth opportunities for the non-automotive businesses, such as services (particularly financial) and aerospace, could be exploited. Daimler-Benz and Chrysler were keen to enhance their financial standing, broaden their access to intellectual capital and increase their strategic options. The merger, theoretically at least, was a good idea. So what were the difficulties?

Problems with the merger

1 **Cultural issues.** Both the Germans and the Americans anticipated problems relating to their respective cultures, such as language and lifestyle differences, but they failed to consider fundamental differences in the operation of their organisations. For example, the Germans were surprised to find American management practices that segregated personnel and inflated management compensation packages that were not tied to performance.

The joining of two distinct corporate identities and brands created a plethora of roadblocks. The merger was a marriage of opposites, forcing together two different cultures and ways of doing business. Chrysler was fast, lean, informal and daring, whereas Daimler prized meticulous attention to detail, structured management and painstaking research.

If mergers are to succeed, dominant players must pay attention to cultural issues. Research to identify the core values of the merging companies can help, enabling firms to recognise both potential synergies and areas in which the corporate cultures may clash. The problem with the DaimlerChrysler merger was that there was little understanding of how to maximise the benefits of diverse organisational cultures. Staff of both firms were increasingly surprised by the seemingly bizarre behaviour of their colleagues during the merger.

2 **Stakeholder issues.** When Daimler-Benz gained control of Chrysler the merger was born not from meticulous planning but from misunderstanding. Three years earlier, Kirk Kerkorian, a Wall Street investor and Chrysler shareholder, made a bid to take the company private. Kerkorian thought that the carmaker's management team would back him, but Chrysler's executives had other ambitions. Led by boss Bob Eaton, Chrysler executives blocked Kerkorian's bid and a battle to control Chrysler ensued. Into the fray came Daimler-Benz as Chrysler's saviour. Soon Daimler and Chrysler prepared to merge in a super-deal that would remodel and redefine both

companies and the automotive industry as a whole; but Chrysler would not admit any form of defeat, steadfastly believing that it was not inferior to Daimler-Benz in any regard. After a management exodus at Chrysler's former headquarters in Detroit, Jurgen Schremmp finally dismissed Chrysler's president. This triggered increasingly nervous Chrysler investors to pursue Schremmp through the American courts for breach of contract, claiming he had previously maintained that the union was a merger and would not involve purges of Chrysler management.

In spite of turbulent management changes and layoffs of over 30,000 people, the Chrysler division continued to perform below par. DaimlerChrysler's share price dropped from a post-merger peak of $108 in 1999 to $43 by September 14th 2001. Instead of the $3 billion in savings expected to result from synergies obtained by sharing platforms and standardising parts, the company was struggling with substantial losses by the start of 2002, three years after the merger.

Substantial efforts were made to explain the deal to shareholders and keep them informed, but other stakeholders, which in this case included regulatory bodies whose approval for the deal was crucial, were often inadequately considered.

3 **Short-term issues.** Attention focused on sealing the deal, not on the longer-term, all-important issue of how to make it work.

4 **Leadership issues.** The leadership at all levels of DaimlerChrysler clashed as the new company drew its leaders from two radically different firms: Daimler-Benz and Chrysler (see point 1 above).

5 **Corporate identity and communications issues.** There are dangers in replacing familiar brand names with those of a new brand. The magic of the old may be destroyed, or at least diminished, by the logic of the new. The degree of emotional attachment felt by stakeholders to a company's name should not be underestimated. In the case of DaimlerChrysler, Daimler-Benz's stakeholders were offended by their company's renaming as they believed the process was really an acquisition, and Chrysler stakeholders were similarly offended by the renaming of their company.

Once a deal is agreed in principle, the chances of it succeeding will be greatly enhanced if the messages sent out from both organisations are consistent. This rarely happens in a thoroughly convincing way, but when it does it makes a big difference.

6 **Potentially conflicting objectives.** It is hard for employees to focus on the corporate objectives of a merger if they are worried about their own position. All mergers involve reorganisation and job cuts, so to keep employees as "on side" as possible there must be regular and honest communication.

There is a powerful case for replacing managers who are opposed to the deal and rigidly attached to bygone organisational values with people better able to lead the new firm. This should be done early on. At DaimlerChrysler, people were made redundant at all levels slowly and tortuously throughout its first three years, thus souring the merger.

So, is big beautiful?
Many commentators, such as management guru Tom Peters, view major mergers such as that between Daimler-Benz and Chrysler as a recipe for disaster. If a firm is strong, then a merger will introduce sources of weakness, or at best take attention and resources away from sources of strength. If a firm is weak, then it is better to focus on the sources of weakness rather than divert resources into negotiating and implementing a merger. There is an argument that rapidly enlarged businesses leave themselves open to leaner, quicker and less bureaucratic competitors.

The counter argument is borne out by the DaimlerChrysler merger. Although success may be difficult to achieve it is still possible to prosper, and despite its many problems, DaimlerChrysler is evidence of this. Furthermore, for many organisations it represents the best, or only, option.

> *Mergers – out of fashion after a decade of behemoth-building deals – may have unfairly acquired a bad reputation, according to a study by the Milken Institute, a California think tank. The research, which examined 276 takeovers by public companies over a 15-year period, found more than two-thirds of the deals led to increased efficiency, as well as savings of about $28 billion overall.*
> Jennie James and Hugh Porter, "Keeping it together", *Time*, August 19th 2002

Although mergers hold a great deal of promise and there are undoubted successes, it seems that negotiating the many pitfalls inherent in such deals – from cultural issues to communications – can be hazardous and difficult. This may not be the fault of the merger; the forces that drive firms to merge in the first place might also place strains on the union over the long term.

After a painful birth, DaimlerChrysler now has strong positions in many markets, opportunities for growth in new ones and a pool of valuable resources, including some of the strongest brand names in the automotive sector. Leaders able to engineer the merger process competently in the future will have a skill that is in great demand and short supply.

Other methods of growth

Non-merger integration

One way to grow that does not involve merging is working more closely with other businesses in the same industry, through partnership deals, joint ventures or strategic alliances. Integration can be vertical, involving organisations in the same industry but at different stages of the value chain (for example, PepsiCo linking up with restaurants that will sell its beverages). Vertical integration can provide businesses with greater control over the whole process of creating goods and or services and getting them to the customer.

In contrast, horizontal integration involves collaboration between organisations in the same industry; for example, a law firm in the United States forms alliances with law firms in many other countries in order to provide a more global service. Horizontal integration can provide economies of scale, as well as enhancing the size, expertise and credibility of both businesses. But to grow successfully through strategic alliances the aims of all those involved need to be similar and clearly understood. The alliance must be structured so that it does not fall foul of antitrust laws and competition regulations, notably in Europe and the United States.

Diversification

Diversification involves a business moving into another area of activity. This can be either a new product in an existing market, for example an airline starting a low cost service, or a new product in a different market, for example an established airline buying a rail franchise and operating train services. Diversification can be achieved with partners, as well as through the introduction of new finance, and can provide a number of benefits:

- Over-reliance, or even dependence, on a small group of customers is removed and risk is spread.
- The existing business can become more attractive, enhancing perception of the brand, customer service and market share.
- Market share in both businesses can be improved, as synergies and marketing offers can be exploited.
- There is some protection against changing fortunes in traditional markets which can result in short-term difficulties or long-term terminal decline.
- The effect of a market exit will be less damaging if you operate in other profitable markets.

Diversification can provide new opportunities for existing skills and spare capacity. For example, an advertising agency may set up a video production company producing corporate videos because it has the necessary skills and resources. This is known as concentric diversification, where existing skills, customers and sales channels are at the core, but the applications broaden in concentric rings.

Specialisation

The opposite of diversification, specialisation involves dropping non-core activities, or even redefining and focusing on core operations. The main advantages are a clear focus and strength in depth, with all available resources channelled into one endeavour. It also means that any cash available from the sale of non-core operations can be used to grow the business.

Reliance on this approach depends on doing what you do sufficiently better than your competitors and on successfully anticipating and adapting to market changes.

The perils of growth

Growth is difficult to manage and it depends on having the necessary cash. Because of the lag between the time investments are made and when they start repaying, it is crucial to maintain the support of financial backers, keeping them informed.

Growth can disrupt existing processes and organisational structures and working methods. If such growing pains are not remedied quickly, they can have serious consequences. The solution is to identify all the things about the current business that work well and must be retained, as well as what needs improving. Explaining plans to customers and suppliers will help allay any concerns that they have.

Competitors may see a change in strategy or structure as an opportunity to attack, perceiving the growth initiative either as a sign of weakness or possibly heralding a period of strength that requires a pre-emptive strike. Competitors may feel stung into action to preserve their market position. Furthermore, growth can signal that the sector is doing well, encouraging competitors to enter the market or broaden their activities. The solution is to keep a close eye on the market – speaking to customers, for example – and to take decisive action in the event of any moves by competitors.

Another problem associated with growth is rising costs, most frequently administration costs, if there is duplication (in the case of

M&A) or if the administrative function becomes overstretched and inefficient. Other reasons for rising costs include over- or under-shooting capacity, with either too much inventory or not enough. In any strategy for growth, it is important to increase awareness of the need for cost control.

Depending on its rapidity and scale, growth will affect corporate culture – everything from innovation to decision-making and team-building – and people may need additional training and support. Needless to say, integrating workforces that perform broadly similar roles yet have large differentials in pay and conditions may prove difficult.

Key questions

The following questions can help when determining a strategy for growth:

- Where are the most profitable parts of the business?
- What are the prospects in the short, medium and long term for those other potentially profitable parts?
- How precarious is the business? For example, does it rely on too few products, customers, suppliers, personnel or distribution channels?
- How clearly focused is the business? Is it overburdened with too many products, markets and initiatives, or is it running on empty with too few opportunities on which to capitalise?
- What is likely to be the best method of expansion, and is it affordable in terms of money, other resources and time?
- What are the advantages and disadvantages of expanding, and what must be done to achieve the benefits and avoid the pitfalls?
- What do people in the organisation see as the best options? What are their views of potential opportunities and difficulties?
- Is there the commitment to act decisively and consistently? Once set, the course needs to be rigorously followed. One of the greatest obstacles to growth is inertia.
- Do you understand how the changes will affect people? If employees feel threatened, disregarded or insecure, then no matter how sensible the decision and implementation it is likely to fail as people will not be sufficiently committed to it.
- What are the success criteria and performance measures? How will these be monitored?

When considering a merger or acquisition the following issues are relevant:

- How does the merger or acquisition fit with the business strategy?
- What are the main issues faced in making the deal a success? In particular, what decisions are needed, and how will they be reached?
- How will the best target be identified and decided upon? Are there other potential targets that would be better?
- How well is the deal structured? Is the price reasonable and likely to provide a realistic return?
- Where can you decide to compromise and what issues are non-negotiable?
- How has the integration of the target business been planned? What are the main priorities and intended benefits, and how swiftly will these be realised?
- How might issues of organisational culture affect the deal? How can you limit any negative effects – or, ideally, build on the cultural fusion?
- Who is responsible for planning and communicating the deal, selling its benefits and establishing the identity and focus of the new business? How will they achieve this?
- Have issues of corporate identity and communication been considered?
- Is the leadership behind the deal ready to make the necessary decisions that will make or break it?

8 Competitive strategy

Businesses generally either dwell on their competitors' activities or ignore them on the grounds that they are unable to exert any direct control. The amount of attention that needs to be paid to competitors varies according to the nature of the industry and market, and usually lies between these two extremes. Decision-makers may be guided by an overall vision and specific objectives, but competitive pressures can also be decisive in determining their decisions.

The impact of competition

Michael Porter has identified five forces affecting competition in an industry, and these provide an interesting lens through which to view current and potential competitors. The five forces are industry rivalry, market entry, substitutability, suppliers and customers.

Industry rivalry

Companies in the same industry – be it banking, car manufacturing, travel and tourism, retailing or whatever – are the most obvious and prominent source of competition. The cola wars fought by Pepsi and Coca-Cola are just one example of this.

When competitors get fizzical: fighting the cola wars

In 1975, Pepsi directly targeted its long-term competitor, Coca-Cola, with the "Pepsi Challenge", claiming that in taste tests people preferred Pepsi. After Coca-Cola conducted its own tests rumours spread that Coke did indeed have a taste problem. In public, Coca-Cola appeared unconcerned. But senior executives knew that they could not afford to ignore Pepsi's latest marketing offensive, given that Coke's market share had fallen substantially in the face of competition from Pepsi and from new beverages such as diet drinks, citrus flavours and caffeine-free colas. Indeed, Coca-Cola, realising that tastes were changing and competition was getting tougher, was itself marketing many of these new products. However, Coca-Cola's taste problem was a serious issue for a core product, and Coke's shrinking lead in the cola market convinced senior executives of the need to act. In the *New York Times*, Brian Dyson, head of Coca-Cola USA, commented:

> *There is a danger when a company is doing as well as we are ... to think*
> *that we can do no wrong. I keep telling the organisation, we can do wrong*
> *and we can do wrong big.*

During December 1984 the company decided to proceed with a new formula for Coke. The target date for the launch of the new formula, new Coke, was April 1985 and Dyson involved Coca-Cola's senior marketing and public relations officials, who were given the vital (and secret) task of co-ordinating new Coke's debut.

New Coke, new problem

Technically, the launch went well. However, even before they had tasted it millions of Americans disliked new Coke. Across the country and especially in the South, the birthplace of Coca-Cola, consumers reacted angrily and emotionally to the new formula. Thousands contacted the organisation's headquarters in Atlanta. Remarkably, many were not Coca-Cola drinkers, simply American consumers disappointed at a major change to an iconic American product.

By mid-July, the pressure had become enormous, and Roberto Goizueta, the chairman, together with other senior executives announced that classic Coke would return. The news was leaked the previous day, and ABC News had interrupted daytime programming to break the story. The next morning headlines were filled with what insiders called "The Second Coming". On the day of the official announcement, Coca-Cola's hotline recorded 18,000 calls. For the first time in over two months people were positive, glad that their voices had been heard and that such a change had been aborted.

The company's executives might have feared the consequences of reintroducing classic Coke, resulting as it did from unhappy customers, bad press and ignominious defeat. But the opposite occurred: it proved massively popular. Against all expectations, classic Coke outsold new Coke, and sales overtook Pepsi early in 1986. Attempting to explain the renewed popularity of classic Coke, senior executives told the *Wall Street Journal*:

> *It's kind of like the fellow who's been married to the same woman for 35*
> *years and really didn't pay much attention to her until somebody started*
> *to flirt with her.*

Although a clever analogy, it masked the total surprise that engulfed everyone at Coca-Cola. No one could explain the renewed appeal of the old formula. New Coke was supposed to be exciting, popular and built upon a century of success, whereas classic coke was thought of as satisfying the traditionalists. By overly focusing on what the competition was doing and on its own market research (designed in the light of what the competition was doing) Coca-Cola had lost sight of the strength of its brand and the unpredictability of the customer. New Coke declined in popularity, shrinking to a 3% market share, and classic Coke began selling with renewed vigour.[1]

The lesson for competitors
Coca-Cola introduced new Coke after taste tests proved it more popular than Pepsi and the original Coke. However, the launch of new Coke contained an untested assumption: that flavour mattered more than image. The information gathered built upon this flawed notion, confirming the decision that classic Coke needed to be replaced. This view was contrary to what customers – past, present and future – actually wanted. Interestingly, this goodwill was so powerful that the cause of the company's failure was also the source of its salvation, as consumers forgave Coca-Cola and realised that they appreciated classic Coke, or else tried it for the first time.

Market entry
New entrants to a market pose a competitive threat that firms under-estimate at their peril. So firms should always think hard about who might enter the market, how and when this might happen, and who has the resources, technical skills and ingenuity to move in on your territory with a more attractive product offer. (This level of understanding and insight can be developed with scenario thinking, outlined in Chapter 6.)

Substitutability
Businesses with a product or service for which customers might choose an alternative face a competitive threat, especially if the alternative is cheaper. For example, an airline may face competition from a high speed rail operator. What matters is recognising that some organisations need only to redefine their business in slightly broader terms for it to become a competitor. This was highlighted in the 1960s by Theodore Levitt, a business writer and marketing guru, who warned of the dangers of marketing myopia: seeing a business in simple, narrow terms, rather than from the perspective of the market. It is important to a business in broad terms that are understood by the market: for example, an airline company is a transport company, and may therefore enter the rail or shipping business; a theatre is in

the leisure industry, and may start competing with cinemas or restaurants, and so on.

Suppliers

Suppliers wield significant power if the item they provide is scarce or unique, or if there are only a few suppliers. They have considerable power to damage a competitive position. One response is to build close relations with important suppliers to secure delivery and control prices. In the long term, the solution may be to move into the supplier's industry to safeguard supplies.

Customers

The power of the customer is another source of competition. The issues that need consideration are how dependent the business is on individual customers, the ease with which customers can move to another supplier, the customer's knowledge of the business's competitors and the conditions (price, quality, overall offer) that are prevailing. The growth of the internet as a sales channel has empowered customers. In an increasingly networked, global marketplace, prices become transparent and it is much easier to discover when prices for the same thing are different in separate geographic markets. Price transparency became even more of a strategic issue for businesses in euro zone countries when they adopted a single currency.

Factors intensifying competition

Decision-makers should be able to recognise when competition may arise or when it is gathering pace. Competition can intensify in several circumstances:

- When a market is expanding or new, as with computers and software over the past 20 years or with the mobile telecommunications industry during the past ten years.
- When the stakes are high and there are big profits (or losses) to be made, notably when there are few organisations in a large market as, for example, with Coca-Cola.
- When a market is about to change, perhaps as a result of developments affecting patents and intellectual property rights (for example, when the patent for a drug expires), or political or legal developments, such as privatisation.
- When a market is shrinking, especially when there is

overcapacity in an industry (usually one that is mature), with firms chasing fewer and fewer customers. This is apparent in a number of long-established manufacturing industries such as ship-building, steel-making and car production.

Building competitiveness

The following checklist provides a framework to ensure decisions help build a firm's competitive strength.

Develop market awareness

Developing a keen sense of market awareness requires keeping up-to-date with what your competitors are doing, how they are perceived in the market, and why. Decisions should take the following into account according to the importance attached to each:

- pricing policies and product offers;
- brand reputation and recognition;
- customers' perceptions;
- product quality;
- service levels;
- product portfolio;
- organisational factors such as size, economies of scale, type of employees, training, expenditure on product development and distribution channels;
- organisational culture;
- staff loyalty;
- promotional campaigns, timing, nature and channels used;
- customer loyalty;
- financial structure and performance and cash reserves.

Build and exploit sources of competitive advantage

Developing and maintaining a keen awareness of the market will help a firm identify its sources of competitive advantage and disadvantage, and then to build on strengths and minimise its weaknesses. There are many ways to do this and tangible and intangible resources that can be used in the process.

- Cash reserves can be used to finance sustained marketing campaigns, innovative development programmes or price reductions.

◪ Purchasing power and the ability to secure reliable supply at low costs develop competitiveness. Costs, quality, prices and delivery can be improved by building close working relations with preferred suppliers.

◪ People are invariably the decisive factor in achieving success: an organisation can only be as good as the people who work for it. If there is typically a high staff turnover in the industry, the business should be geared to recruiting the best employees. If flexibility and speed of response are valuable (and they usually are), the organisation should be able to anticipate major decisions, making the right choices and implementing them. Effective leadership is essential; its absence is a source of competitive disadvantage.

◪ Product factors inevitably have a significant impact on competitiveness. They include pricing and discounts, distribution channels, marketing methods, brand reputation and appeal, product quality and how the product relates to others (for example, the popularity of film merchandise rests largely on the success of the film).

◪ Market awareness – understanding who the customers are and what they want (and do not want or need) – is also decisive in determining competitiveness. Few markets are clearly defined, and although a business may be open to any potential customer, it is important to know exactly who the core customers are so that their interests can be given priority.

Understand the issues affecting the organisation's competitiveness

A strategy may be well conceived and executed, and it may even succeed in achieving its aims, but it may still be vulnerable to a competitor's actions. To be robust, decisions need to take account of potential competitive threats, and so it is useful to consider worst-case scenarios to make decisions.

Consider the example of a small sandwich bar with a regular, local clientele. Suddenly, a film crew comes to town and, because of its exclusive patronage, business booms. Is this good for the sandwich bar? In the short-term, definitely. In the longer term, possibly not. Regular customers may go elsewhere, tired of waiting longer than usual to be served, and when the film crew leaves, the sandwich bar will be in a weaker position than it was before they came, if its original customers have discovered better or cheaper competitors. One solution may be to deliver orders (or at least the film crew's), and have more pre-prepared sandwiches to minimise delays. A more desperate and less satisfactory measure might be (after the film crew has left town) to reduce prices or increase marketing with the extra cash made during the boom. In any event, market awareness is vital to competitiveness.

The fast and the furious: competing in difficult times

Air France, in common with other established carriers in Europe and North America, found its traditional markets threatened by the downturn in the airline industry and the increase in low-cost carriers. To remain competitive, the company paid special attention to four techniques:

- **Reacting rapidly.** All Air France's main decisions following the crisis of September 11th 2001 were taken on September 18th. They were later adjusted and developed, but the new strategy was formed and implemented quickly.
- **Acting collectively.** The board meets to react quickly, considering how best to respond to events and how to co-ordinate their response.
- **Constantly looking at all competitors.** This keeps the business lean and focused on what matters. In France, there has been an established lower-cost competitor to Air France since 1981: the TGV high-speed train. This has meant that many of the disciplines needed for competing with low-cost operators have been developed over many years.
- **Using all available resources.** Competing has meant employing all the assets and advantages that a big industrial carrier has in order to counter low-cost operators, including its brand, market position and operational strengths. Often a competitor's strategy is to build market share with temporary low prices and then to raise them. An active and patient approach can help to reduce or remove the threat of competitors.

Be a SWOT

SWOT (strengths, weaknesses, opportunities and threats) analysis is most effective and beneficial when it forms part of an overall management audit. It can be done from the top, or each department or division can conduct a SWOT analysis of its operations which is then reviewed at departmental or divisional level and themes and conclusions are developed. The results can be assessed alongside a larger picture of the

Table 8.1 **Sources of strength and weakness**

Financial issues	People issues	Operational issues	Product and market issues
Cash flow and cash management	Quality (meaning the ability, experience and attitude) of managers and employees	Current product portfolio	Warehousing, transport and logistical factors
Financial structure	Concentration of skills and expertise (to what extent is the fate of the business in the hands of a talented few?)	Research and technical expertise, and the ability to develop popular new products	Distribution channels, including discount structures and dealership or franchise operations
Financial reporting systems	Levels of motivation	Market research systems	Pricing
Ability to raise capital	Rates of pay	Information management systems	Brand perception
Credit-control activities	Ability to attract and retain the best people	Supply chains	Customer service
Risk-management systems	Scope and effectiveness of training methods	Production lead times and efficiency	Overall market potential for the product
	Flexibility of people and their ability to adapt to changing situations	New processes that reduce costs and increase efficiency	Experience of the marketing mix (knowing which sales activities are most effective)
	Organisational culture: does it promote efficiency or frustrate it?	Stock control	
	Organisational structure: is it still relevant and effective?		
	Levels of delegation and empowerment, and productivity in terms of quality and quantity of work completed		
	The degree of initiative that is both allowed and taken		
	Levels of pressure (a strength) and stress (a weakness)		
	Effectiveness of communication channels		

Table 8.2 **Sources of opportunity and threat**

Opportunities	Threats
New markets (including export markets)	Industrial action
New technologies	Political and regulatory developments
New products and product enhancements	Economic issues
Mergers, acquisitions and divestments	Trade factors
New investment	Mergers and other developments among competitors
Factors affecting competitors' fortunes	New market entrants
Commercial agreements and strategic partnerships	Competitors' pricing actions
Political, economic, regulatory and trade developments	Competitors' market innovations
	Environmental factors
	Natural disasters
	Crises, notably including health and safety issues, product quality issues, product liability problems
	Key staff attracted away from the business
	Security issues, including industrial espionage and the security of IT systems
	Supply chain problems
	Distribution and delivery problems
	Bad debts (resulting from the misfortunes of others)
	Demographic factors and social changes affecting customers' tastes or habits

market that takes into account current and potential developments for the whole organisation.

Strengths and weaknesses are typically found within an organisation whereas opportunities and threats are most often outside it. Some factors can be sources both of strength and weakness. Take the age of employees, for example. Older employees may denote a stable organisation able to retain employees and maintain a wealth of experience, or it may simply mean that the organisation is too conservative. Some of the most common areas of strength or weakness are detailed in Table 8.1. All of these can be either strengths or weaknesses, and they often change from one to the other surprisingly quickly.

External factors are more difficult to assess than internal ones. Examples of sources of opportunities and threats are detailed in Table 8.2.

Key questions

Assessing an organisation's competitiveness is a complex, demanding and continuous task. What matters is the ability to create in the organisation an atmosphere of acute awareness of the market, where people sense developments and signals and possess the ability to act on them. Consider the following questions:

◪ How effectively does the business sense developments in the market? Market sensing goes well beyond market research. At its core is a determination to derive unique insights into the needs of customers and the opportunities within markets. It includes:

All actions, formal and informal, systematic and random, active and passive, engaged in by all members of an organisation which determine and refine individual or collective perceptions of the marketplace and its dynamics.[2]

◪ How well does the business translate market insights into competitive advantage? Understanding customers and their shifting needs is difficult. Employees close to the market should be encouraged to develop their insights by:
  - emphasising informal rewards;
  - co-ordinating the work of different departments;
  - influencing the views, values and overall approach of managers in the organisation;
  - fostering a healthy disregard for industry norms and encouraging experimentation and learning;
  - promoting trust and openness among individuals so that information and ideas are shared and discussed in an apolitical manner.

- What are the main sources of competition (for example, is it industry rivalry, substitutability or something else)?
- How effectively are competitors monitored? Who decides how and when to respond to competitors, and how effective have those responses been in the past?
- How competitive is your industry, and what is the trend (more competition or less)?
- How competitive is your organisation, and most importantly, how does it compare with others in the eyes of the customer?

The next chapter builds on these issues, focusing on techniques for ensuring that commercial decisions reflect market realities and customers' needs.

9 Customer focus

Understanding customers, market developments and technology leads to customer-focused decisions and these, in turn, provide the most certain route to profitability. However, to realise these benefits requires a keen understanding of where a market is heading and how opportunities can be exploited. It is easy to dismiss customer-focused decision-making as self-evident, whereas in reality it is often difficult to incorporate customer issues accurately into decisions. Techniques that help managers achieve this include:

- Market sensing
- Market segmentation
- Data mining
- Using the internet for decision-making
- Product development

Market sensing

The value of technology in bonding with customers, building loyalty to products and brands, and improving customers' knowledge of products and services is immense. It can also increase understanding of market developments, that is, market sensing. The key to competitiveness these days is to know what each individual customer wants, as opposed to the broad generalisations about (often arbitrary) market segments made only a few years ago. Internet systems and customer databases can help, if they are intelligently designed and used.

Analysing customer data from loyalty schemes and special-offer promotions can inform decisions that benefit both the business and the customer. Loyalty schemes, such as those provided by supermarket chains like Tesco in the UK and Migros in Switzerland, or airlines' frequent-flyer programmes generate individual-level purchase data. These data can be invaluable in helping determine the most effective strategy, improving the effectiveness of strategy by, for example, highlighting which customers account for the greatest proportion of profit.

Individual-level data are valuable when introducing a new product. Aggregate sales figures show whether the product is a success at the moment, but an analysis of trial rates (percentage of customers who have bought the product once) and repeat rates (percentage of customers who have bought the product at least a second time) is needed to reveal the long-term prospects for the product. Estimates of trial and repeat rates are often used in deciding whether to introduce a product at all. This kind of data is particularly important in retail environments, where it is easy to obtain through barcode scanners.

Using market sensing for customer focused decisions requires:

- **Using market research objectively.** Market research needs to be well designed, executed and interpreted. Flaws in the way that people think when making decisions, outlined in Chapter 3, can mean that research simply validates a proposed approach: it is subjective rather than objective. Research can be used to satisfy political agendas rather than to create insight about the market. The best approach is to use research to refine and update your understanding of customer groups.
- **Using research insights to identify unique qualities.** Insights should provide a source of competitive advantage – a scarcity value – that competitors are unlikely to have realised. The research needs to be cross-referenced, pursued, interpreted and enriched with accumulated knowledge and understanding to provide real insights.
- **Being in touch with customers at a senior level.** Decision-makers must be in touch with customers, seeking opportunities to meet with them formally and informally. Customers usually welcome the opportunity to have their voice heard and this simple measure informs the views of senior managers.
- **Anticipating the future.** Managers should develop foresight through scenario thinking. As discussed in Chapter 6, this involves engaging stakeholders, including customers, in thinking about future scenarios and, most significantly, what factors might bring these scenarios or something similar into reality.
- **Involving all employees.** To achieve the best possible understanding of market issues, there must be an organisational structure, climate and practical process allowing everyone to share their knowledge of customers and to use these insights to improve customer service. Customer focus is not for the few, it is an essential prerequisite for everyone.
- **The alignment of information systems.** Information systems need to be aligned so as to provide a clear and coherent

understanding of customers' preferences and actions. Perhaps surprisingly, many companies' IT systems do not support detailed reporting about customers, to the extent that some global businesses cannot easily determine who their 20 largest clients are measured by sales or profitability. Lack of data is a major handicap in understanding customers and building a clearer understanding of the market.

Leadership matters

The role of leaders in developing market-sensing capabilities is highlighted by Sean Meehan, a professor at IMD business school:

> In the end, senior management really does have to decide how much creating customer value really matters. Their job is complex and the resources competing for time and attention are many, so they need a guiding light and vision. In the case of the leading software company Intuit, everyone is guided by "do right by the customer". This genuinely matters and thus it is likely that the organisation will have the right mindset, and will do what is necessary to align itself to create customer value. It will then routinely ensure that investments in market sensing produce an appropriate return.[1]

Market segmentation

Market segmentation involves profiling a target market in order to understand, in as much detail as possible, how best to sell and deliver customer service. One benefit of segmentation is that it enhances product development. Another is the ability to understand customers and their buying habits, making marketing plans relevant, targeted, well implemented and cost-effective. Segmentation also influences pricing strategies, providing a more detailed understanding of customers and markets.

Conventionally, segmentation breaks information into sections relevant to the target market. Applying different criteria (such as income, location and age of consumers) to a market generates tightly focused information. The internet is a valuable tool for segmenting markets. It enables decision-makers to understand the organisation and composition of the market, target potential customers, build the loyalty of existing customers and analyse information to improve marketing efficiency. As the internet provides access to markets that are global, diverse and complex, market segmentation allows greater focus and simplicity.

Types of segmentation

Markets can be segmented into any group. The most appropriate divisions depend on such factors as the size and nature of the market and product, as well as the reason for segmenting the market. The following categories are often used.

- **Commercial markets.** Categories are commonly divided into Standard Industry Classification (SIC) codes. For example, customers may be given a range of SIC codes (relating to job title, industry sector, location, company turnover). These are then used for specialised targeting of subgroups (for example, all project managers in the oil industry in Scotland with a company turnover of more than £10m). Useful segments include geographic location, type of organisation, job title, size of organisation and purchase data.
- **Consumer markets.** The most common segments are geographic location, product benefits, lifestyle and social groupings. The internet is useful in determining the segment that will value a product. Other segments include occupation, income, nationality, sex and age.

Data mining

Data mining is the gathering of information about customers, with the aim of analysing and then using it in the most effective ways.

Scientifically accurate market segmentation depends on data mining. One of the values of the internet is the ability to capture and use information relating to every customer transaction made through it. For example, internet retailers such as amazon.com use data to customise their business services. Dell.com uses information from sales to ensure future offers are appealing and competitive; and during the technology boom of the late 1990s, Dell reported industry-leading revenue from its website of $15m per day.

Collecting information

Computer systems are used widely to record and analyse every part of the transaction between businesses and their customers. In using technology in this way, the following principles should be followed.

1 **Decide what information to collect.** It is important to avoid drowning in information about customers that is of little or no real use. Work out what information is desirable and focus on collecting it in order of importance. For a shoe firm, shoe size will be crucial, whereas head size will be of no use at all unless the shoe firm is planning to diversify into hats. Work out where more than one set of data needs to be assessed before a conclusion can be drawn. This interrelation of information is important when analysing data that has been aggregated from a range of sources. The focus for information collection needs to be on building better one-to-one relationships with individual customers. With data mining, the objective is to provide an information engine that will drive the organisation so customers receive a continuously improving service.

2 **Decide how best to collect the data.** Data collection requires a sophisticated approach. It may involve just a few simple, easy-to-answer questions, but it may depend on them being asked at the right time. For example, when a customer has decided to buy online and is at the order screen, provide them with payment options asking how they would prefer to pay, or whether they would be prepared to pay a premium for delivery. Competitions are another popular method of gathering data, as are online surveys.

3 **Test the effectiveness of data collection.** The process of data collection may seem logical and necessary, but does it seem so to the customer? Will customers think they are being asked questions that are time-consuming, annoying or pointless? If so, the cost of acquiring some marginally useful data may not be worth it. There may also be obvious questions such as "How can we improve our service to you?" that are going unasked, so it helps to consider the obvious before attempting to be too clever. There are three simple rules for data collection:

- Put yourself in the customer's place.
- Keep it as simple as possible.
- Apply common sense.

4 **Ensure that information is kept up-to-date.** It is tempting to rely on historic data, and it is always interesting to review the development of trends over time. However, it is much more useful to ensure that data is current and accurate. One of the main reasons websites have grown in scope and popularity, with virtually every major organisation now

possessing at least one, is that they offer speed and flexibility when dealing with customers. They are also a valuable source of information.

Analysing information

Database vendors provide tools that allow analysis of information contained in a database, using a query. The process can be automated for large organisations that need to analyse or respond to information quickly, perhaps across a large volume of customer records (airline reservation systems or online bookstores are prime examples). Furthermore, queries can be combined using "and" or "or" commands to identify complex relationships within sets of data; this in turn can be used to identify key issues, opportunities, concerns and trends.

Aggregated data can be used to identify the preferences and habits of groups of customers, as well as data about a specific customer's preferences. Aggregate data is most useful at the macro strategic level. Individual data is more powerful at the micro level of strategy implementation as it can be used to build a more compelling, customised offer for individual customers.

Loyalty schemes favoured by organisations from airlines to supermarkets exploded in popularity, only to lose their competitive impact within a few years. Part of the reason was that customers learned that the rewards of loyalty were usually small and often uninteresting.

Using customer data

The value of detailed market and customer information is enormous. Common uses of customer data include the following:

- Tracking purchasing habits. This can show how frequently customers buy, how much they spend, how they choose to make their purchases and, perhaps most importantly, what they are choosing to buy. Information about buying preferences enables organisations to start building genuine, practical relationships with their customers, increasing the likelihood of repeat business. It also allows them to target products at the customers most likely to buy them.
- Enhancing special offers. Analysis of special-offer promotions may reveal that the organisation does not need to discount prices. This in turn can remove the "wasted" margin that may occur when the price of a product is reduced to attract people that

would be prepared to buy it at the higher price. Analysis may show that the people that would value the product are the ones hearing about it.

- Maximising sales opportunities, leading to repeat business and increased revenue at marginal cost. Linked with the previous benefit is the ability to increase customer response rates through improved targeting. This occurs when a current or potential buyer of one product is targeted with another complementary one. So, for example, if a customer is viewing cars online, an advertisement for a financing package may appear.

- Developing new sources of revenue. Detailed customer data may highlight new, unknown or previously difficult to exploit business opportunities. For example, an online travel agency may have previously avoided selling ancillary products, from insurance to sun-cream, but given the potential new scale of their business and the ability to sell ever more effectively to a wider range of people, new product offerings may prove worthwhile.

Using the internet for decision-making

There are many ways to develop new products or boost the profitability of existing ones using the internet. The principles for online innovation are, with several additions, similar to those for offline product development (see Table 9.1).

The internet and customer-focused decisions

One of the most significant business benefits of the internet is the ability to create new relationships with customers. This includes the ability to capture, store and disseminate detailed information about customers and their preferences, thus allowing swift and practical decisions on everything from new product development and pricing to stock levels and future marketing plans. It enables faster, more reliable transactions, improving efficiency and reducing costs.

The internet also enables different scenarios to be tested, thus enhancing the accuracy of decisions. Another advantage is the ability to provide special-offer promotions offering significant value. As well as facilitating the promotion, the internet also enables customer data to be analysed and used to inform future decisions.

Customer relationship management

The use of technology to store, analyse and disseminate information is

Table 9.1 **Developing products via the internet**

The challenge	*The action required*
Understanding customers' priorities and market realities	◪ Research customers' views: request information, provide incentives for the customer to help shape your product. ◪ Research competitors in the same industry and in other industries, understanding different business models and critical success factors. ◪ Meet customers and get them to understand your business. It is never too early to start building trust and loyalty online.
Finding ways to improve and innovate	Improvements are achieved by: ◪ Looking for new ideas and ways of improving business operations. This may be achieved by putting yourself in the customer's position or looking at other businesses and industries facing similar issues. ◪ Brainstorming when conditions are right. Brainstorming can occur under pressure, perhaps as part of a problem-solving process, or it may take place ad hoc, in response to a particular issue or situation. ◪ Involving people at all levels in the organisation. When innovating, few things are as frustrating as a constant raft of initiatives lacking priority, resources or leadership. A new approach may be needed that: – establishes a clear process for new developments; – gives innovation a profile among top-level leaders; – facilitates knowledge-sharing; – ensures that best practice expertise is shared; – invites and then acts on customer comments.
Hiring and retaining talented people	◪ Adopting a flexible, imaginative approach to recruiting and then retaining talented staff. A premium is often placed on people with experience of doing things a particular way, when what often matters more is a "can-do" approach, combining an understanding of what is possible with what is important. ◪ Providing people with incentives to generate ideas and implement them.
Streamlining business processes	◪ Reviewing existing processes from the customer viewpoint can help to deliver greater profitability. Understanding what works best and what customers want will count for nothing if it is not effectively implemented.

not only enabling swifter decision-making, but it is also opening up new opportunities for building better and more distinctive relationships with customers. Information about customers' preferences and behaviours is being captured, and this is not just happening online. Retail stores, having introduced scanner technology to make transactions much quicker and more reliable, have found themselves with enormous databases of transactions that can be useful for decision-making. Many organisations accumulate online data, but only some (the successful ones) use it to increase profitability.

Clickstream data

There are two sales challenges when developing an effective website: to produce a site that collects relevant data in a way that will not deter customers; and to analyse the data and integrate it into development and sales decisions. Collecting data online typically starts when people visiting a site for the first time are asked to register, giving a name, physical address, e-mail address and usually some other demographic data (such as age or income). From the customer's perspective, this is all that needs to be done. Once this process is in place, the business has to ensure that the website is secure and personalised for each customer, using as much of their personal data as possible. This is used to provide an appealing site, targeted at the interests and needs of individual customers. When customers revisit the site, it is possible to learn more about them by recording their series of "clicks", the information they request using their mouse. Clickstreams allow behavioural information to be added to the other data that are collected.

Personalisation online

The implications of personalisation for consumers are enormous. Consumers generally do not mind being asked to part with information in order to receive a personalised product or service, and positively value what they perceive as a benefit. However, it is worth bearing in mind the experience of one business that tried to leverage new technology to personalise its service. It went too far, and using data collected online telephoned customers with a sales pitch emphasising a disconcerting amount of personal information. Consumers reacted negatively, offended by what they considered an invasion of privacy.

The implications of personalisation for businesses are also extensive. Internet and especially e-mail advertising are regaining some of their popularity, as advertisements are viewed by specific, targeted groups.

Treating customers as individuals is now becoming much more prevalent, and the personalisation that is developing on the internet will have far-reaching consequences in the offline world too. This is because customers' expectations are influenced by their online experiences. In a study in 2000 by Jupiter Communications, a research firm, 35% of executives surveyed said that personalisation capabilities were the most important factor when choosing who should develop their website. It is worth considering that in one vital respect the internet is much more like radio than television. Although it has a global reach, the internet has the one-to-one intimacy of radio as well as the mass appeal of broadcast TV. The advantage of this intimacy – or closeness to customers – is that corporate decisions are then more easily able to reflect customer priorities.

Product development

New product development can be fast or slow, reactive, adaptive or proactive, but it is always hazardous. This section examines the forces influencing product-development decisions, focusing on major decision points in the product-development process.

Product-development decisions will take into account market trends, competitors, customer needs and the size – and priority – of available opportunities. Factors internal to the organisation will include strategic goals and the long-term positioning of the business, the strength of the business's reputation and product portfolio, and the cash available for developing new products or product extensions.

Knowledge and innovation: the development of the credit card

The word innovation conjures up the image of a process that is spontaneous and unpredictable, even unmanageable. Innovation literature abounds with stories of serendipitous discoveries and independent-minded champions doggedly pursuing an idea until they hit the jackpot. Often, as the stories don't fail to stress, the inventors had to persist in secret in their labs without the knowledge or against the will of senior colleagues. The archetypes of such innovators are Art Fry and Spence Silver, the 3M chemists who turned a poorly sticking adhesive into a billion-dollar blockbuster: Post-it notes. In most of these stories, innovation comes from the labs or marketing outposts, not from the top of the organisation. In this situation, the role of management, in the view of Lewis Lehr, a former CEO of 3M, is "to create a spirit of adventure and challenge".

However, the role of senior managers in developing innovation is often more significant and direct, and it relies on the support and use of information and knowledge. The commercial development of the credit card is an example. In 1958, researchers in the Customer Services Research Department at the Bank of America, with the remit to develop potential new products, created the first credit card. This development was augmented later by seven bankers at Citibank who added the key features of credit cards, including merchant discounts, credit limits, and terms and conditions.

The credit card did not result from a market need; it emerged because people within the banking business used their tacit knowledge. This included their sense of the market and understanding of customers; information and forecasts about economic and social trends; experience with similar product ideas (such as instalment loans); and knowledge about new technological developments. It heralded the beginning of innovation within the retail financial services industry, and led to such developments as ATM machines and the growth of telephone and internet banking.

There are three points to note about the credit card which distinguish it from the more famous bottom-up and serendipitous innovations such as the Post-it note.

- ◪ The support of senior managers was essential. They set up the unit, helped to develop it and provided the support it needed to take root and grow. Indeed, in 1977 Citibank innovated in this sector again, this time with a marketing drive to increase its share of the lucrative market for credit cards in the United States. With a single mailshot to 26m people, it became, virtually overnight, the largest issuer of Visa and Mastercards in the world. This enabled the bank to strengthen all its activities, and it eventually became the world market leader in retail banking. This level of innovation required top-level support.
- ◪ Senior managers were particularly significant early in the process, creating the right conditions and providing support and momentum.
- ◪ Information is at the heart of top-down innovation. Managing information and tacit knowledge is an essential part of ensuring that the innovation process starts, continues and delivers success. (The value of knowledge for product development and innovation is explored further in Chapter 10.)

Decision points

In arriving at product development decisions the following provides a framework of what to take into account.

Market issues. Understand the market as clearly and accurately as possible:

- Define customers' needs and identify which features of the product will be most appealing.
- Determine, in as much detail as possible, who the product appeals to and why.
- Consider market trends, including price, customer expectations and technological developments.

Organisations need to understand their existing and potential customers, and find ways to connect with them. To do this may involve market sensing techniques explored earlier in this chapter.

Innovations can arise from experience, creative genius or by collaboratively adapting the work and ideas of others. Learn from others by considering how everything from market research to developing customer loyalty has been addressed in other markets or industries. An understanding of current and future sources of competition will also guide development decisions.

Product issues. It is necessary to consider the overall product portfolio, assessing how a new product fits with existing ones and how well it supports the organisation's overall strategy. (For example, whether the organisation is positioning itself as a high-value provider of premium-value services, or whether it is more concerned with high volumes and low costs.)

Resource issues. Issues relating to production, personnel and operations often receive less attention during development decisions than external factors relating to customers and competitors. However, it is essential to consider such questions as:

- Are the processes, skills and resources in place to develop and sell the product?
- How can financial viability and in particular the profit margin be enhanced?
- Are costs likely to fluctuate?
- How reliable are suppliers?
- How will the desired quality standards be achieved consistently?
- How can the level of risk be reduced and the return on investment increased? (This is explored further in Chapter 11.)

Managing channel conflict

For businesses selling through different channels – direct, online, via agents or retail outlets – conflicts can arise unexpectedly, and the various sales channels should be evaluated during the product development process. This means assessing the value, significance and potential of each channel. The most profitable ones should be maintained, and those with potential should be nurtured. Ensuring that each channel has a slightly different value proposition is a prerequisite to maximising their advantages. This may require targeted sales initiatives focused on the needs of each market segment.

Key questions

Market sensing

Assessing market sensing capabilities can highlight both where and how the organisation can improve. Consider the following issues:

- To what extent does an informed, dynamic view of the market guide managers' actions?
- How effectively does customer information flow around the organisation? Is there an accurate, consistent and shared understanding of customers: who they are and what they want?
- Is there an overemphasis on gathering and measuring data at the expense of action? (The danger of data infatuation.)
- Is market data merely used for political purposes, justifying predetermined courses of action?
- Do market insights guide major decisions?
- How unique are the customer insights that are influencing your organisation? Are they easily available to your competitors?
- How comprehensively do you monitor competitors' actions?
- Are competitors seen from the customers' viewpoint?
- How creative is your organisation in its response to customer data? What would improve it?

Market segmentation

- Are your markets segmented in a way that reflects the current market?
- Are your market segments clearly focused and simple, or do they need to change?
- To what extent are customers and competitors considered when making decisions? Could this be improved?

Data mining

- ◪ Does your organisation collect, analyse and use all of the available data?
- ◪ Is information kept up to date?
- ◪ Are customers contacted consistently and are senior managers actively involved?
- ◪ Are information systems able to provide a clear understanding of customers?

Using the internet for decision-making

- ◪ Does your website provide maximum decision-making value?
- ◪ What is the trail from customer information captured online to decisions being made? How could this trail be enhanced?
- ◪ How is the internet being used to refine advertising effectiveness? Could more be done in this area?
- ◪ Would clickstream data enhance understanding of customers?
- ◪ Are adequate safeguards in place to protect the security of customer information, and to ensure that customers are not overwhelmed by requests for information?
- ◪ Personalisation and special-offer promotions are activities that can both inform decisions and add value for customers. Are these techniques being successfully applied?

Product development

- ◪ What will make the product unique or valuable to customers?
- ◪ Which benefits will be used to sell the product?
- ◪ How, where and by whom will the product be sold?
- ◪ What will be the pricing strategy?
- ◪ What sales volumes can be expected?
- ◪ Where are the likely difficulties and danger points?

10 Knowledge and information

Knowledge is the intellectual capital that an organisation possesses. It is much more than data, as it includes the experience and expertise found within an organisation. Information is generally objective, whereas knowledge includes elements of interpretation and understanding. Technological developments have prompted an explosion in the scope and depth of knowledge to which decision-makers have access. However, there is now so much information and knowledge available that what sets successful organisations apart is their ability to develop and use them creatively.

Knowledge and information have to be collected, protected and effectively and intelligently managed if they are to be valuable resources that guide and inform every stage of decision-making. There is increasing recognition of the benefits of using not just some but all employees' knowledge, by developing simple and robust systems that allow information and expertise to flow to key points in the organisation. When information is withheld or poorly managed, it often causes suspicion, frustration or resentment. However, introducing systems to control and direct information can be disruptive, causing additional work and pressure.

Managing knowledge and information

Many organisations rely on technology, data flows and processes, but in ways that can reduce – or at best, fail to take advantage of – the wealth and utility of knowledge individuals possess. Avoiding this situation is the focus of knowledge management. Several techniques for effective knowledge management are outlined below.

Undertaking a knowledge audit

Few firms really know what knowledge they possess, often because it is confined to a few or simply neglected. A knowledge audit is designed to uncover the breadth, depth and location of an organisation's knowledge, and it has three core components:

- Defining what knowledge assets exist, especially information or skills that would be difficult or expensive to replace.
- Locating those assets; that is, discovering who keeps or "owns" them.

- Classifying them and assessing how they relate to other assets. In this way, opportunities can be found in other parts of the organisation.

Increasing knowledge

The results of a knowledge audit allow an organisation to use and develop its knowledge and information to support the strategy of the business. The challenge is to increase the knowledge base, which can be done in three main ways:

- Knowledge can be bought; for example, by hiring staff, forming alliances and partnerships or outsourcing.
- Knowledge may be rented by hiring consultants or subcontracting work.
- Knowledge can be developed through training and continuous learning.

An organisation's website can be used to expand, refine and enhance new sources of information (see Chapter 9).

Maintaining knowledge

Knowledge gaps make an organisation more vulnerable to competition. The downsizing strategy that many firms have followed has highlighted the dangers of getting rid of people with expertise and experience in the pursuit of short-term cost savings. Furthermore, traditional employee loyalty is continually being eroded, as described in Chapter 1, so it is important to capture, codify and store people's expertise and tacit knowledge.

Protecting knowledge

Because knowledge is often an important source of competitive advantage, it is essential to protect it. Knowledge falls into two categories: explicit knowledge, such as copyright or information codified in handbooks, systems or procedures; and tacit knowledge that is retained by individuals, including learning, experience, observation, deduction and informally acquired knowledge. Explicit knowledge can be protected through legal procedures, and although tacit knowledge can to some extent be protected by legal methods (such as non-compete clauses in employment contracts), it is sensible to ensure that valuable tacit knowledge is recorded and passed on.

Establishing information systems

An efficient information management system will co-ordinate and control information and will help with planning. There are three main stages in developing a system:

- Decide what information is needed, perhaps preparing a wish list of what will help improve decisions and achieve objectives. Information can be categorised by type, such as customer information, financial details and staff information. Note that certain pieces of information may fit more than one category.
- Understand when information is required and who needs it. Too much data produced too frequently can result in information overload, making it harder to discern trends or relevant details. Knowing who requires each piece of information involves assessing how information flows through an organisation. Often information flows according to status, from the top to the bottom, along the channels of the organisation chart. This has inherent weaknesses as some people may require more data, or more time with the data, than others do.
- Consider how best to display the information. It needs to be clear and accessible: too much information is distracting and too little is inadequate.

In addition to the above you need to:

- Ensure security of information. Confidential data should be secure and information should be backed up to avoid valuable information being lost. Back-up files or documents should be held in a different location.
- Manage costs and provide the necessary support. To gain maximum value from investments in information technology, list the functions and features that are required (including price and support) to ensure that minimum requirements are fulfilled.
- Make data available for shared use throughout the organisation. Any problems or concerns that may prevent this happening need to be resolved.
- Be aware of legal requirements and their implications, particularly relating to data held on customers, suppliers and employees. These requirements are increasing in scope and complexity.

◪ Establish guidelines to avoid misuse or misinterpretation of data (see Chapter 3 for thinking flaws relating to the use of data and information).

Managing the flow of information

In order to maximise the usefulness of any information system, it is valuable to understand how information flows, what it is used for and the ways in which it can be applied.

Understanding information requirements. To identify information requirements and to make information routinely, consistently and reliably available, ask the following questions:

◪ What information is needed?
◪ How should it be presented (for example, online, with written approval, occasionally, informally, in meetings, by memo)?
◪ When does it need to be supplied (timing and frequency)?
◪ Where does it come from? This can determine the quality of information, as well as relevant details that put the facts into context.
◪ What restrictions are there? For example, is some or all of the information confidential?
◪ Which decisions and activities will it support? It can help if people see why the information is needed.

Acquiring the right data. Information should be reliable and useful. There are many techniques for acquiring it, including surveys, telephone calls, meetings and interviews, and there are sources such as libraries and information centres. All provide insight if used intelligently. Customer surveys can be carried out online and the web provides a valuable source of regularly updated information. The appropriate technique depends on the nature of the decision that is to be made.

Reviewing and analysing information. By reviewing and analysing information, options emerge and their effectiveness can be assessed. In the end, decisions come down to judgment, but quantitative statistical methods will highlight trends and anomalies, and scenario planning, modelling and simulation (explored in Chapter 5) are useful techniques for generating and assessing information.

Storing and retrieving data. Information should be widely accessible, and clearly labelled and categorised. It should be relevant and up-to-date, and this means establishing criteria for adding new information and discarding (or archiving) old, irrelevant details. Lastly, the system and processes for storing and retrieving information should be cost-effective.

Acting on information. Three tactics are useful when using information:

- Monitor decisions. See how well a decision is being implemented, and assess whether new decisions are necessary and the implications for future choices.
- Act methodically. This matters, because if the method is flawed so may be the resulting decision.
- Managing constraints and other pressures. Keep a firm eye on objectives even in the light of tight deadlines and the need to make fast, focused decisions.

Information orientation

Given that many billions of dollars are invested each year in IT software and hardware, you would expect managers to know how information technology and their information systems improve their organisation's performance. However, research indicates that managers are largely unaware of what they need to do to ensure that investments in information and knowledge deliver bottom-line improvements in performance.

Donald Marchand, of IMD in Lausanne, and William Kettinger, director of the Centre of Information Management and Technology Research and information systems professor at the Moore School of Business at the University of South Carolina, conducted research at IMD business school that identified three critical factors driving successful information use. These factors combine to provide an overall measure of information orientation (IO).[1] It is often said that you cannot manage what you cannot measure. Marchand emphasises that you cannot measure what you cannot see, and how managers see the world defines their actions and what they are able to achieve. Unfortunately, many managers see the use of information only within the narrow context of technology. However, technology and information in isolation do not create sustainable competitive advantage.

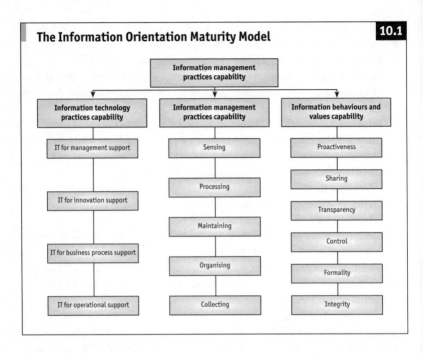

The Information Orientation Maturity Model `10.1`

This view is potentially toxic for the major suppliers of customer relationship management (CRM), enterprise resource planning (ERP) and other software systems, which are often promoted as the technological panacea for whatever ails an organisation. According to *CIO Magazine*, up to 70% of CRM projects will not produce measurable business benefits.[2]

The three capabilities of information orientation
Statistical research involving over 1,000 senior managers from 98 companies in 22 countries demonstrated the existence of three information capabilities: the organisation's information behaviours and values, information management practices and IT practices. These three capabilities contain 15 specific competencies (see Figure 10.1).

The three information capabilities combine to determine how effectively information is used for decision-making.

- ◪ **Information behaviours and values.** This is the capability of an organisation to instil and promote behaviours and values for effective use of information. Managers should promote integrity, formality, control, transparency and sharing, removing barriers to information flow and promoting information use.

▪ **Information management practices.** Managing information involves sensing, collecting, organising, processing and maintaining information. Managers set up processes, train their employees and take responsibility for the management of information, thus focusing their organisations on the right information. They take care to avoid (or at least minimise) information overload, improve the quality of information available to employees and enhance decision-making.

▪ **Information technology practices.** IT applications and infrastructure should support decision-making. Consequently, business strategy needs to be linked to IT strategy so that the IT infrastructure and applications really do support operations, business processes, innovation and decisions.

Interestingly, Marchand and Kettinger found that companies with multiple business units do not always build the same levels of IO across the entire company. The new IO measure is being used by an increasing number of international corporations and governmental organisations, and provides a useful framework for managers in building strategic IT capabilities.

Avoiding disorientation: information orientation at work[3]

Several companies have successfully implemented major IT projects including Banco Bilbao Vizcaya Argentaria (BBVA), Spain's second largest and Latin America's largest bank, SkandiaBanken, Sweden's first branchless bank, and Cemex, a Mexican cement producer that has become the third largest in the world.

BBVA transformed its failing branch-based retail banking business into one of the most successful banks in Spain in 1,000 days. This was accomplished by getting the right information to people in the branches, enabling them to successfully cross-sell their products. BBVA kept its new customer relationship project simple by providing its customer representatives with:

▪ An easy-to-use and intuitive IT interface.
▪ Clear information about customer segmentation, product selling targets and company performance information.
▪ Team-building incentives, to create an open culture emphasising teamwork and action.

SkandiaBanken created a model for online business that has been profitable and has surpassed larger institutional competitors in customer service and value. The managers of SkandiaBanken, a pure internet and telephone bank, attribute their success to a business model that integrates simple IT infrastructure and web solutions, easy information access for customers and employees, and a company culture stressing transparency, personal responsibility and a bias for action.

Cemex transformed its small commodity business in Monterey, Mexico, into the third largest cement company in the world. It has outperformed Holcim and LaFarge, its international rivals, in share price, operating margins and return on assets. Cemex has a reputation for building satellite networks and using IT to monitor and control kiln temperatures in any plant in the world from its headquarters in Mexico. Furthermore, it uses GPS technology to guarantee delivery of ready-mix cement within a 20-minute window. Cemex managers admit that its success was based on a cultural change that emphasised a proactive approach to meeting commitments, using information to develop new ways of serving customers, and developing information-centric processes that provided more efficient operations.

Managing information so that decisions are as effective as possible depends upon people: how they use available information and systems, how they share their knowledge with others and how motivated they are to use information to innovate and create value. It also depends on the processes used to manage information and knowledge. The technology itself, although essential for success, is just a tool that has to be used intelligently and skilfully if it is to do the job required. The IO measure, with its broader, rigorous assessment of the information capabilities in an organisation, provides a transparent and tangible framework for managing all aspects of information effectively.

Organisational learning

New ideas are essential to improving organisations. They may come from flashes of creative brilliance, from other industries or from a simple analysis of new information. Whatever their source, new ideas are the essence of improvement. Ideas are central to making the right decisions, solving problems and adding value for customers. The way that organisations can achieve this is by efficiently applying knowledge and information. Those that do are learning organisations, defined as:

> *An organisation skilled at creating, acquiring and transferring knowledge, and at modifying its behaviour to reflect new knowledge and insights.*[4]

It is in this last part of the definition, the need to modify behaviour, that so many organisations fail. Those that do manage to live up to the whole definition have shown huge improvements in overall performance, largely by transforming the way in which knowledge is used. They include Honda, General Electric, Corning and General Motors' Saturn Division.

"Organisational learning" is presented as a powerful technique to improve performance, especially in turbulent times. In business, "learning" is generally used in the context of organisations' attempts to improve efficiency and effectiveness and to be more innovative in uncertain market conditions. The greater the uncertainty, the greater is the need for learning. Arie De Geus who worked for Shell for many years before becoming a business academic, suggests that in the long run survival depends on decisions displaying a sensitivity to the environment and flexibility. This is embodied in an organisation's ability to learn, to experiment, to continually explore new opportunities to create new sources of wealth and value, and to change its behaviour to fit what is happening around it.

The view of David Kolb, a management writer, is that the learning process consists of four stages: concrete experiences, reflective observation, abstract conceptualisation and active experimentation. Furthermore, the process is an iterative one. Learning begins with observing what has occurred, reflecting on what has been observed and assessing the underlying structures that drive the behaviour we observe. From this we develop a theory about what is happening, and this theory influences the development of a decision. These actions set an expectation. However, invariably reality will deviate, drawing our attention to what is different from our expectation. This initiates the next iteration of the learning cycle: reflection, conceptualisation and mental model building. This learning is not an episodic event: it is a continuous process. Reflection and action combine to produce learning. Without action there can be no learning, as all that we can then reflect on is our previous reflections.[5]

Organisational learning occurs when the learning cycle is performed collectively in the organisation. This is when people reflect on their experiences, collectively developing new theories based on observation and then acting together. In the process of joint reflection, there is a sharing of individual views leading to a shared understanding. According to Kees van der Heijden:

The cycle of learning 10.2

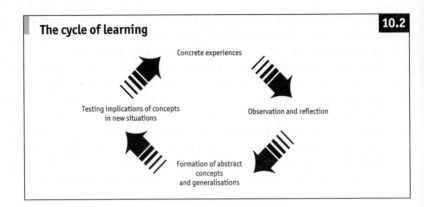

If a critical level of alignment of mental models takes place within the organisation, planning effectively becomes a joint activity, and experiences will be common, leading to joint reflection in the group and reinforcement of a shared mental model.[6]

Therefore without joint action, organisational learning cannot occur. A similar observation comes from Henry Mintzberg:

Study after study has shown that managers work at an unrelenting pace, that their activities are characterised by brevity, variety, and discontinuity, and that they are strongly oriented to action and dislike reflective activities.[7]

The orientation to action and dislike of reflective activities are reinforced by organisational cultures and reward systems, which tend to encourage action and work against managers who wish to pause and reflect. Managers must be seen to be doing things. Sitting around thinking is perceived as being idle, even though spending time thinking about how you can build competitive advantage and profits is clearly essential. Action and reflection are therefore essential for organisational learning.

Getting started
Changing an organisation's culture and the way it functions takes time, but the following steps will help to turn an organisation into a learning one:

- Foster an atmosphere conducive to learning. Give managers time to pause and reflect, to use their knowledge to generate new insights and ideas, and above all, to learn. This process of learning tends to be driven out by pressures and stress.
- Stimulate the exchange of ideas by reducing bureaucracy and boundaries. In most organisations, structures, hierarchies and boundaries inhibit the flow of information, keeping individuals and groups isolated and reinforcing preconceptions. Emphasising communication and opening up the organisation lead to fresh flows of ideas, competing perspectives and insights. Jack Welch, former CEO of General Electric, views "boundarylessness" as one of the most potent forces for change.
- Create learning forums. Once managers are working within a supportive, stimulating environment, they can create opportunities to foster learning, by enabling people to wrestle with new knowledge and consider its implications. A learning forum can be anything from a strategic review or benchmark report to a visit to customers or a supplier.

These steps are just a start. Any action – such as using appraisals to engender support and enthusiasm for learning – that removes barriers to learning and promotes action-centred learning will result in improved decisions and actions through better knowledge and understanding.

Key questions
- Does useful information flow freely and easily through the organisation to the people that need it and can use it to greatest effect?
- How well is information used for decision-making? Are there examples of failings that could have been mitigated with more effective use of knowledge and information?
- Would your organisation benefit from a knowledge audit – a methodical assessment of where critical knowledge lies within the business? For example, which individuals hold the most valuable knowledge, such as understanding customers' needs?
- Is the website adding to the organisation's knowledge base? How might information collection be enhanced?
- How well does your organisation use IT to support management, innovation, business processes and operations?
- How successfully does your organisation sense, process,

maintain, organise and collect information? Is this assessed, and could it be improved?

- Is information used in your organisation proactively? Is it shared, transparent, controlled and formalised, with its veracity and integrity protected?

11 Managing finance and risk

Managers routinely consider issues of profitability, cash flow, long-term shareholder value and risk when setting and reviewing strategy. This chapter provides practical guidance relating to financial decisions and explains:

- the value of ratio analysis, explaining how to apply techniques for ratio analysis in decision-making;
- techniques for improving profitability, such as break-even analysis;
- how to avoid pitfalls in making financial decisions;
- techniques for reducing financial risk.

Applying ratio analysis

Ratio analysis not only supports the assessment and definition of decisions, it also helps to monitor them and avoid inappropriate or damaging actions. Its role is threefold: to analyse; to monitor and measure performance; and to facilitate future plans. Ratio analysis is often used to support systematic analysis of suppliers, customers and competitors, as well as general market and industry trends.

When using ratios ask the following questions:

- Which ratios are most appropriate for each part of the business? Masses of irrelevant ratios waste time and cause confusion. Knowing which ratios apply to different areas improves the efficiency and focus of analysis. An awareness of which ratios other people monitor allows the broader organisational picture to be kept in sight. Taking time to communicate to the people affected by decisions how each ratio works and what it means in practice keeps strategy focused and people committed.
- What does the ratio mean? Is it absolute (for example, the number of days' credit taken by debtors) or relative (such as the level of gross profit)? What lies behind the ratio figure(s)? For example, what are the causes behind the trend?
- How reliable are the data on which the ratio is based?
- What comparisons are desirable in using a ratio? Ratios are most effective when compared over time or between competitors.

Plotting ratios in charts illuminates trends, as well as clearly communicating the data.

Ratios are used across a wide spectrum of business activities, from marketing or managing people to production. For managers, the most significant ratios relate to markets, assets, providers of capital, suppliers and employees. Some ratios are described below.

Ratios relating to markets and products

Sales growth. This is measured by dividing sales for the period by sales for a previous period. The period that is chosen can be highly significant: the shorter it is (a day or week), the more sensitive the ratio becomes. Shorter periods are more relevant for reflecting seasonal demand.

Value of work in hand. This highlights the size of a firm's order book. It is calculated by dividing the value of orders in hand by the average value of daily sales. Analysis of this ratio over an extended period highlights trends in sales performance: large fluctuations may indicate instability or vulnerability.

Marketing efficiency (sales to cost ratio). This is calculated as a percentage of revenue and is marketing spend divided by revenue. When budgeting, for example, it is useful to know how much money needs to be devoted to marketing to generate a given level of sales.

Market share. In highly competitive situations, sales growth should be read alongside the market share ratio. This is calculated by dividing current market share by previous market share. If market share is being taken together with sales growth, the periods need to be similar.

Ratios of the market share of each product, or the product as a percentage of turnover, can be compared between periods to see how markets and product groups are developing. This highlights strengths and weaknesses in a product portfolio and can be used to gauge a product's position in its life cycle. If it is declining, it is important to decide if it is a long-term and irreversible trend or a short-term blip that you can take action to reverse.

Liquidity and other commercial ratios

Gross profit and net profit ratios. These two ratios reveal much about the profitability of a business. The gross profit ratio indicates the profitability of sales once direct costs of sale are deducted, and the net profit ratio highlights the overall effect of all costs in relation to gross profit. The gross profit ratio is calculated as gross profit (revenue less direct costs of sales, that is, excluding overhead costs) divided by revenue. Each industry has its own standards and norms for gross profit and, as with any ratio, it is important to monitor and control fluctuations in gross profit over time. The net profit ratio is calculated as net profit (revenue less total costs) divided by revenue. Ideally both ratios should increase over time as the business becomes more established but, as markets become more competitive and crowded, margins get squeezed.

Gross profit can be related to product lines. Net profit can also be related to product lines if overheads are allocated appropriately.

Creditor and debtor days. Creditor days measures the number of days on average that a company pays its creditors. Debtor days (also known as accounts receivable days) is the reverse: the number of days on average that it takes for a company to receive payments. Debtor days matters because it provides an indication of a firm's efficiency in collecting monies owed.

Creditor days are calculated by dividing the cumulative amount of unpaid suppliers' bills by sales, then multiplying by 365. Debtor days are calculated by dividing the cumulative amount of accounts receivable by sales, then multiplying by 365.

Debtors to creditors ratio. This shows the relationship between the credit given to customers and the credit received from suppliers. It is calculated by dividing credit given by credit received.

Quick (or acid-test) ratio. This is an assessment of a company's liquidity, showing how quickly a company's assets can be turned into cash, which is why it is known as the quick ratio or simply the acid ratio. The most common expression of the quick ratio (although there are several ways of deriving the same result) is to subtract inventory from current assets, and then divide this by current liabilities. In general, the ratio should be 1:1 or better, reflecting a healthy proportion of current assets to current liabilities.

Stock turnover. This indicates how long cash is being tied up in stock. It is calculated as the stock value divided by the average daily cost of sales. The quicker stock turns over the more efficiently cash is being used.

Profit vulnerability. The vulnerability of profits to increasing costs can be monitored by dividing fixed expenditure (for example, fixed overhead costs such as premises or salaries) by total expenditure. This identifies where costs are changing and which costs are causing fluctuations in profitability over time.

Ratios and providers of capital
Price/earnings (P/E) ratio. The price/earnings ratio is simply the share price divided by the earnings per share (EPS). It is the one that investors and analysts focus on and it forms part of the valuation of a company during acquisitions and disposals. The higher the ratio, the more the company is deemed to be worth, although there are several points to note. P/E ratios vary across industry sectors and in different countries, and are relative to those of competitors. They rise when the share price rises – for example, when there is speculation about a merger or takeover. They can also lag behind events, combining current share price with past earnings. A P/E ratio may, for instance, be too high compared with likely future growth.

Return on equity. One of the principal tests is how much money a business makes for its investors, who therefore pay considerable attention to it. It is calculated as net profit after tax divided by equity capital.

Ratios and suppliers
Suppliers' prices and performance can be monitored using ratios. Fluctuations in prices are measured by dividing a supplier's current prices by its prices at a previous date. The time that suppliers take to deliver is calculated by dividing the value of outstanding orders with suppliers by the value of average daily purchases. An indication of a supplier's reliability can be obtained by dividing the value of overdue orders from the supplier by the average daily purchases from all suppliers.

Ratios and employees
Productivity can be measured in a number of ways. Profit per employee is calculated by dividing profit by the number of employees. A more interesting ratio of value-added per employee is calculated by dividing sales minus materials costs by the average number of employees.

Employment costs can be measured and monitored for a range of criteria. For example, training costs can be related to profit for budgeting purposes by dividing profit by training expenditure.

Improving profitability
Entrepreneurial flair is as much a state of mind and attitude as it is a set of skills. Nonetheless, certain skills will ensure that decisions are entrepreneurial and focused on commercial success.

Variance analysis
However diligently a budget is prepared, things will not turn out as planned. There will be a variance between what was anticipated and what happened. Understanding the differences between actual and planned performance is known as variance analysis. It is useful to analyse such variances in order to understand why things are going better or worse than expected and act on the lessons learned.

The process starts by breaking down substantial variances into their component parts, identifying exactly where and why the variance occurred. For example, small variances in unit costs or unit prices will have substantial effects on the bottom line in a mass volume business. Key performance indicators (KPIs) can be used to track and identify variances and areas where the firm's performance is deviating from expectations.

Common causes of variances include inefficiency, such as poor cost control, poor or flawed planning (for example, relying on historically inaccurate information), poor communication and random factors. Variance analysis is something that every business should undertake but in a practical and pragmatic way that is cost-effective.

Market entry and exit barriers[1]
The ease and difficulty of both market entry and market exit are crucial factors in high-level strategic decision-making. Entry barriers include the need to compete with businesses that are enjoying economies of scale or that have established, differentiated products. Other barriers include capital requirements, access to distribution channels, factors such as technology or location, and regulations imposed by governments or industry associations. When markets are difficult or costly to enter and easy and affordable to leave, firms can achieve high, stable returns while still being able to leave to pursue other opportunities. Consider where the barriers to entry lie for your market sector, how vulnerable

you are to new entrants and whether it is possible to strengthen and entrench your market position.

Break-even analysis (cost-volume-profit or CPV analysis)

Knowing when a project or new business will break even is important in any decision to invest money, time and resources in it. Break-even point is when sales cover costs, where neither a profit nor a loss results. It is calculated by dividing the costs of the project by the gross profit at specific dates, making an allowance for overhead costs. Break-even analysis is used to decide whether to continue development of a product, alter the price, or provide or adjust a discount, or whether to change suppliers in order to reduce costs. It also helps with managing the sales mix, cost structure and production capacity, as well as forecasting and budgeting.

For break-even analysis to be reliable, the sales price per unit should be constant, as should the sales mix, and stock levels should not vary significantly.

Controlling costs

Focus on major items of expenditure. Costs should be categorised as major or peripheral items. Undue emphasis is often given to the 80% of activities accounting for 20% of costs, rather than focusing on the priorities: the activities generating the majority of costs.

Reduce costs through cost awareness. While focusing on major items of expenditure, it may also be possible to reduce the overall level of cost of peripheral items. Costs can be reduced over the medium to long term by influencing people's attitudes towards cost and wastage. In particular, examine managers' attitudes to cost control and reduction and the effects of expenses on cash flow and profitability.

Maintain a balance between costs and quality. Commercial management and cost control mean getting the best value possible. This requires a balance between price paid and quality received.

Use budgets for dynamic financial management. Budget early so financial requirements are known as soon as possible. Consider the best time-period for the budget. This is normally a year, but it depends on the type of business. Budgets can be of interest to people outside the business as well as providing a starting point for cash-flow forecasts. They are also useful in monitoring costs.

Develop a positive attitude to budgeting. People need to understand, accept and use the budget, and to feel a sense of ownership and responsibility for developing, monitoring and controlling it.

Eliminate wastage. For decades, leading Japanese companies have directed much of their cost-management efforts towards *muda* or waste elimination. This involves techniques such as process analysis, mapping and re-engineering, which are important parts of operational decision-making. The value of process analysis is that it enables waste to be identified and eliminated and costs to be reduced by thinking of activities as a chain of events from the beginning of the process to the end, with each part of the chain comprising discrete, identifiable tasks. The idea of thinking about everything that goes on in a business in terms of processes and waste elimination is fundamental. In a Japanese factory, you can see how processes have been laid out and almost feel the continuing search for better ways of doing things in the least wasteful way.

Rough riders: Harley Davidson and Caterpillar's routes to profitability

Harley-Davidson, a motorcycle manufacturer, hit hard times during the late 1970s that resulted in a management buy-out in 1981. At this point, senior managers visited Honda's Marysville, Ohio, motorcycle facility. The contrast with their own facility was dramatic in terms of layout, production flow, efficiency and inventory management. Harley's managers concluded that if they were to compete with Japanese motorcycle manufacturers, they would have to effect a business-wide, just-in-time manufacturing initiative. They called it MAN: materials as needed. Production operations were moved together, reducing the resources required for materials handling. Managers were also able to reduce the quantity of inventories received (and produced) too early and the amount of space required for manufacturing. As it later turned out, they were creating space for additional production.

Caterpillar had a similar experience. During the 1980s, Caterpillar's managers concluded that the company's cost structure was significantly higher than that of its principal competitor Komatsu, a Japanese firm. Caterpillar was moving parts and partially finished products from one production area to another, whereas Komatsu was using more of a "flow" process. Caterpillar's managers undertook a significant plant rearrangement initiative called PWAF (Plant With a Future). This led to their own flow process, with a marked reduction in distances between operations, material handling expenses, inventory levels and cycle time to produce products. In some cases, cycle time was reduced as much as 80%.

Improving profitability

Some of the most useful practical techniques to improve profitability are as follows:

- Focus decision-making on the most profitable areas. Concentrating on products and services with the best margin will protect or enhance profitability. This may involve redirecting sales and advertising activities.
- Decide how to deal with the least profitable products. These often drift, with dwindling profitability. Decisive action is needed to turn around a poor performer. You can reduce costs, raise prices, alter discounts or change the product; or you can abandon it altogether to prevent a drain on resources and reputation.
- Ensure that new products enhance overall profitability. New product development often focuses on market need or the production process, with insufficient regard to the financial issues of cost, price, sales volume and overall profitability, which are inextricably linked. Interestingly, for certain products in certain markets, lower prices may reduce demand.
- Manage development and production decisions. The amount spent on research and the priorities and methods used affect profitability. Too little expenditure may result in larger costs in the long term. The shelf-life and appeal of a product should be considered when deciding whether to continue production or not. The number and quality of suppliers are also important. Decide what the buying policy should be (for example, will you have a small number of preferred suppliers or a bidding system among a larger number of potential suppliers). Consider techniques for controlling delivery charges, monitoring exchange rates, improving quality control, reducing stockholding and improving production lead times.
- Ensure that customer decisions improve profitability. Stepping back from routine decisions and considering how to derive greater value from existing customers and products may enhance profitability. Questions to consider include:

- How can customer loyalty (and repeat purchasing) be enhanced?
- How can the sales proposition be made more competitive? (Simply improving it may not be enough; this improvement needs to be made relative to the opposition.)
- How can existing markets, sales channels, products, brand reputation and other resources be adapted to exploit new markets and new opportunities?
- How can sales expenses be reduced?
- How can the overall effectiveness of marketing activities be increased?

◪ Consider how to increase profitability by managing people. Active, successful leadership is a prerequisite to profitability. People need to be motivated and supported. This implies rewarding them fairly for their work, training and developing them, providing a clear sense of direction and focusing on the needs of the team, task and individual.

There are numerous techniques for improving profitability; below are some of the most significant. The most effective approach is the one that best suits the needs of the business, combining entrepreneurship with good leadership and constant financial awareness.

Discounted cash flow and investment appraisal decisions[2]

Discounted cash flow is based on one key principle: that the value of money changes, effectively reducing with time. In other words, cash today is worth more than cash promised in the future. For example, it is not worth investing $100,000 today for the promise of the same amount returned next year; more usefully, discounted cash flow can show that it may not even be worth investing $100,000 today for the promise of $110,000 in three years' time and explain why. There are three reasons for this:

◪ The organisation investing the $100,000 is bearing a market risk, and risk demands return. The greater the risk, the greater is the return required.
◪ Investors are bearing an opportunity cost – they cannot invest the same money in another venture – and this cost also requires return.
◪ Perhaps most significantly, the value of investors' money is being

reduced by inflation, and this also demands a return. If annual inflation is running at 2.5%, then someone investing $100,000 will need a yield after tax of $2,500 a year, just to compensate for inflation. This is central to the concept of the time value of money.

There are five principal steps in discounted cash flow analysis:

1 Develop as accurate as possible a projection of the future operations in which the money is going to be used or the operation of the project, taking into account sales, costs and other relevant financial issues. Typically, the projection should be broken down for each year of the period of the investment.

2 Quantify positive and negative cash flows for each year of the projection, and the annual net totals of cash inflow or outflow.

3 Estimate the value of the cash flow for the final year of the projection. A conservative and prudent approach that is widely adopted is to assume that the final year's cash flow will continue in perpetuity.

4 Decide the discount factor: the percentage that will be deducted from each year's cash flow. Determining this is central to the whole exercise. A higher discount factor will generate a lower overall valuation. Typically, two things influence the level of the discount factor. The first is the level of business risk. If the risk is high (and the investment is unlikely to meet its projections), the discount factor should also be high. Second, there is often a compromise between the cost of borrowed money (such as 5% interest) and the return expected by the investors (for example, 15%); in this case, the discount factor would be 10%. It may be desirable to select a range of discount factors, providing optimistic, realistic and worst-case scenarios.

5 Apply the discount factor to the net cash flow for each year of the projection and to the terminal value. The figures resulting from these calculations are the present value contribution of each year's future cash flow; adding these values provides a total estimate for the value of the investment.

Discounted cash flow analysis is used to help value the potential of an organisation and in making other investment decisions. The discounted cash flow method assesses the projected stream of economic benefits (such as cash flow, net sale proceeds, value of intangible assets) and calculates the maximum investment that should be made. This is known as net present value analysis. It also enables comparison of an investment amount with a stream of economic benefits and provides an overall rate of return. This is known as internal rate of return analysis, enabling analysts to assess the rate of return provided by a particular investment. Many consider that discounted cash flow analysis is more useful than other valuation methods, such as price/earnings ratios. If an investment case is sound, then discounted cash flow will highlight this.

Avoiding pitfalls

Financial decisions affect everyone. They should not be left entirely to the "experts" in the finance department or among specialist advisers. Financial issues and techniques – such as dynamic cost management, the importance of cash flow and the time value of money – affect all managers with a financial responsibility and are influenced by everyone.

Make financial expertise widely available

Every manager in the business should understand the importance of financial management for profitability and success. People need to feel ownership of their part of the process of financial control, to have the information and expertise to make the best financial decisions and to consider all relevant decisions from a financial perspective.

Consider the impact of financial decisions

Do not ignore or underestimate the wider impact of a financial decision on other parts of the business.

Avoid weak budgetary control

Budgets are often used merely to assess performance, whereas their real value is as an active tool to inform financial decisions. Budgets should not be cut without giving sufficient thought to how this will affect other decisions.

Understand the impact of cash flow

Issues of cash flow and the time value of money are often ignored by non-financial managers, to the detriment of the organisation. In the worst case, this may result in the business becoming insolvent.

Know where the risk lies

Understanding where risks lie and what needs to be done to reduce risk is an important part of the process of financial decision-making. For example, you need to know not only where the break-even point is, but also how and when it will be reached.

Reducing business risks

Reducing the risk inherent in business decisions is rarely a linear process. Instead, it is best achieved by applying principles and techniques appropriate to the specific situation and risk. Several of these techniques are outlined below.

Understand and accept risk

The acceptance of risk is an integral part of business, as is the principle that the higher the risk, the higher the rate of return needs to be. The willingness to take risks of both a personal and a financial nature is one of the defining characteristics of the entrepreneurial decision-maker. Interestingly, a 1999 study commissioned by PricewaterhouseCoopers concluded that whereas in continental Europe strategies are generally oriented towards avoiding and hedging risk, Anglo-American companies view risk as an opportunity, consciously accepting the responsibility of risk management as necessary to achieving their goals.

Successful decision-makers understand this. They take steps to ensure that the risks resulting from their decisions are measured, the likely consequences are clearly understood and the danger signals are identified. Avoidable risks are pinpointed and eliminated, and others are reduced. Such decision-makers also take a holistic view of risk, going beyond the direct financial perspective and actively managing risk as it affects the whole organisation.

Accepting that risks exist provides a starting point for other necessary actions. Foremost among these is the need to create the right climate for risk management. People should understand why control systems are needed. This requires communication and leadership so that standards and expectations are set and clearly understood.

Consider the amount of risk

An early step is to determine the risk appetite and risk-bearing capacity of the organisation. In other words, articulate the nature and extent of the acceptable risks. This must be done in the context of the environment in which the business operates, assessing the likelihood of risks becoming reality and the effect that these would have. Only when this is understood can appropriate measures be taken to minimise the incidence and impact of such risks.

Identify and prioritise risks

It is also sensible to be aware of and take into account the human dimension. People behave differently and inconsistently when making decisions involving risk. They may be exuberant or diffident, overconfident or overly concerned. Or they may simply overlook the issue of risk.

One important priority is to identify significant risks within and outside the organisation and allow these to inform decisions. This makes it easier to avoid unnecessary surprises. Examples of significant risks might be the loss of a major customer, the failure of a principal supplier or the appearance of a significant competitor.

Risk surrounds us all the time. As Harold Macmillan, a former British prime minister, once said: "To be alive at all involves some risk." Some of the most common areas of risk affecting business are summarised in Table 11.1. It is valuable when attempting to identify risks to define the categories into which they fall. This allows for a more structured analysis and reduces the chances of risks being overlooked.

To this list should be added another, intangible category: the opportunity cost associated with risk. In other words, avoiding a risk may mean avoiding a potentially huge opportunity. There is a tendency for people to be too cautious and risk averse, even though they are often at their best when facing the pressure of risk or deciding to take a more audacious approach. It is also worth considering that sometimes the greatest risk of all is to do nothing.

Understand the catalysts that cause risks to be realised

Once risks are identified they can be prioritised according to their potential impact as well as the likelihood of them occurring. This helps highlight not only where things might go wrong and what their impact would be, but how, why and where these catalysts might be triggered. There are many potential risk catalysts. Five of the most significant types include the following:

◪ **Technology.** New hardware, software or system configuration can trigger risks and place new demands on existing information systems and technology. When in 2003 Ken Livingstone,

Table 11.1 **Areas of organisational risk**

Financial	Commercial	Strategic	Technical	Operational
Accounting decisions and practices	Loss of key personnel and tacit knowledge	Marketing, pricing and market entry decisions	Failure of plant or equipment	Product or design failure, including failure to maintain supply
Treasury risks	Failure of commercial partners (eg licensees, agents, joint-venture partners)	Acquisitions decisions	Infrastructure failure Accidental or negligent actions (eg fire, pollution, floods)	Failure to develop new products
Financial viability of debtors and strategic suppliers	Failure to comply with legal regulations or codes of practice	Market changes affecting commercial decisions (due to customers and/or competitors)		Client failure
Fraud	Contract conditions	Political or regulatory developments		Breakdown in labour relations
Robustness of information management systems	Poor brand management or handling of a crisis	Resource-building and resource allocation decisions		Corporate malpractice (eg sex discrimination)
Inefficient cash management	Market changes			Political change
Inadequate insurance				

London's first directly elected mayor, implemented a policy of congestion charging for traffic using the centre of the city, the greatest threat to the success of the scheme, and his tenure as mayor, was posed by the use of new technology. Fortunately for London and Livingstone the technology worked, and the scheme was widely seen as a success.

- **Organisational change.** Risks are triggered by, for example, new management structures or reporting lines, new strategies and commercial agreements (including mergers, agency or distribution agreements). The complexity of this risk is illustrated by UK retailer Marks & Spencer's expansion into overseas markets. Unhappily for its managers and shareholders, the strategy failed to deliver the anticipated results. When this was combined with pressures in its core markets, significant measures were needed to get the company back on track (see Chapter 3).
- **Processes.** New products, markets and acquisitions cause process change, and this can trigger the occurrence of risks. Coca-Cola's launch of new Coke outraged coke drinkers and non-drinkers alike, who were angry about such an iconic American product being changed. Although always seen as a high-risk strategy, it turned out to be an even bigger risk than anticipated. The company's ability to turn the situation to its advantage showed that risk can be managed and controlled, but such success is rare (see Chapter 8).
- **People.** New personnel, a loss of key personnel, poor succession planning and poor people management can lead to dislocation. However, the main cause of dislocation within this category is behaviour: everything from laziness to fraud and exhaustion to simple human error can be catalysts, resulting in risk being realised. An example is the financial scandal that ruined Barings Bank during the mid-1990s, resulting from the actions of one rogue trader in Singapore.
- **External environmental factors.** Changes in regulations and political, economic or social developments affect strategic decisions, bringing to the surface risks that may have lain hidden. A good example is the sudden and tragic arrival in 2003, mainly in Asia, of the SARS epidemic, which adversely affected economic confidence and performance throughout the region.

Use a simple risk management process

The stages of managing the risk inherent in decisions are simple. First, assess and analyse the risks resulting from the decision through a systematic process of risk identification and, ideally, quantification. Second, consider how best to avoid or mitigate risks. Third, take action to manage, control and monitor the risks.

Risk assessment and analysis. It is harder to assess the risks inherent in a business decision than to identify them. Risks that lead to frequent losses, such as an increasing incidence of employee-related problems or difficulties with suppliers, can often be overcome using past experience. Unusual or infrequent losses are harder to quantify. Risks with little likelihood of occurring in the next five years do not hold much meaning for a company trying to meet shareholders' expectations in the next quarter, half-year or year. But it is always valuable to quantify the potential consequences of identified risks, and then define courses of action to remove or mitigate such risks.

The risks in each of the categories mentioned above can be mapped both in terms of likely frequency and potential impact, with the emphasis on materiality. The potential consequences of risk may also be ranked on a scale ranging from inconvenient to catastrophic.

Avoiding and mitigating risks. When mitigating risks, start by reducing or eliminating those that result only in cost, essentially non-trading risks. These might include property damage risks, legal and contractual liabilities and business interruption risks, and can be thought of as the "fixed costs" of risk. Reducing these can be achieved with techniques such as quality assurance programmes, environmental control processes, enforcement of employee health and safety regulations, installation of accident prevention and emergency equipment and training, and security to prevent crime, sabotage, espionage and threats to people and systems. Of course, if you reduce the risk, the cost of insuring against it (in cases where you are able to) should go down.

Other ways of reducing or mitigating risks are to share them with a partner, monitor each risk, or make contingency plans in case the risk becomes reality. For example, service agreements with vendors are essential to reduce risk. Joint ventures, licensing and agency agreements are also different ways of mitigating risk.

To minimise the chances of things going wrong, it is important to focus on the quality of what people do: doing the right things right reduces risks and costs. Actively managing and using information is also crucial. Risk management relies on accurate, timely information. Management information systems should provide details of the likely areas of risk and of the information that is needed to control risks. This information in turn must reach the right people at the right time, so that they can investigate and take corrective action.

Assessing and mapping risk 11.1

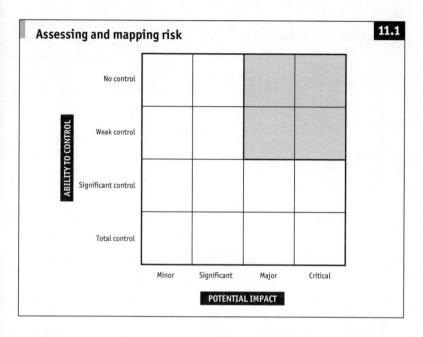

Risk management and control. Experience shows that risk must be actively managed and accorded a high priority, not only within the decision-making process but permanently and throughout the organisation. This might mean that risk-management procedures and techniques are well documented, clearly communicated and regularly reviewed and monitored. In order to manage risks, you have to know what they are, what factors affect them and what their potential impact is.

If the ability to control the risk is plotted against its potential impact, as shown in Figure 11.1, you can decide on actions either to exercise greater control, or to mitigate the potential impact. Risks falling into the top-right quadrant are the priorities for action, although the bottom-right quadrant (total/significant control, major/critical impact) should not be ignored as management complacency, mistakes and a lack of control can lead to the risk being realised.

Once the inherent risks in a decision have been understood, the priority is to exercise control. This essential part of the risk management process builds on the need to ensure that all employees are aware that unnecessary and unsanctioned risk-taking is unacceptable. They should understand what the risks are, where they lie and what their role is in controlling them. To exercise control over identified risks, it is sensible to

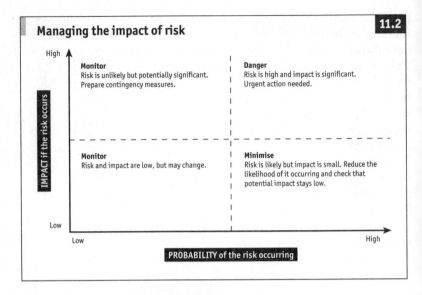

Managing the impact of risk   11.2

IMPACT if the risk occurs — High / Low

Monitor
Risk is unlikely but potentially significant. Prepare contingency measures.

Danger
Risk is high and impact is significant. Urgent action needed.

Monitor
Risk and impact are low, but may change.

Minimise
Risk is likely but impact is small. Reduce the likelihood of it occurring and check that potential impact stays low.

PROBABILITY of the risk occurring — Low / High

share information, prepare and communicate guidelines, and establish control procedures and risk measurement systems.

Create a positive climate for managing risk

Simply recognising the need to manage risk is not enough. The ethos of an organisation should recognise and reward behaviour that manages risk. This requires a commitment by senior managers and the resources (including training) to match. Too often, control systems are seen only as an additional overhead and not as something that can add value by ensuring the effective use of assets, the avoidance of waste and the success of key decisions. A survey by PricewaterhouseCoopers of 100 American companies with revenues of between $250m and $30 billion revealed that more than half of their managers believed controls got in the way of getting work done. In short, it seems that control systems are often seen as getting in the way of people doing their jobs, rather than things that help make sure they don't do their jobs badly.

Overcoming the fear of risk

Risk averseness still predominates in business. Everyone accepts that risks need to be taken if you are to keep ahead of the competition. The answer seems to be a better understanding of what the real risks are, for people to genuinely share responsibility for the risks being taken, and for them to change their own mindset, embracing risk as an opportunity not a threat.[3] Although this conventional approach to managing risk prevails, it is not the whole story. Understanding how organisations manage risk effectively is valuable, but managing risk is only one possible strategy. Another approach is to look for ways to use risk to achieve success, by adding value or outstripping competitors or both. To do this, organisations should stop taking the fun out of risk, emphasising the need to control it in a way that is often perceived as bureaucratic and stifling. As any entrepreneur will tell you, risk is both desirable, providing new opportunities to learn, develop and move forward, and necessary, compelling people to improve and effectively meet the current of challenge and change.

Conclusion: managing commercial risk

To manage the risk inherent in commercial decisions requires an awareness of what the risks are and the danger signals that risk is becoming reality. This is the starting point: in making any major strategic choice you must be confident that you can detect and absorb any potentially dislocating events.

Providing sufficient resources to avoid, mitigate or control risks is important, as is clear organisational communication. Focusing on the quality of what people do is crucial too. Designing and maintaining management information systems to produce the right information in the right form at the right time to the right people should make it easier to control risks, particularly at times of change. Following a process for managing risk involves assessing potential catalysts, avoiding or dulling them and taking action.

But decisions should positively embrace risk. Just as the previous chapter highlighted the nature of organisational learning and how action is central to reflection, development and learning, so audacity is also necessary if progress is to be achieved.

Key questions

- Are the most effective and relevant performance measures in place to monitor and assess the effectiveness of financial decisions?
- Have you analysed key business ratios recently?
- Is there a positive attitude in your organisation to budgets and budgeting?

- Is decision-making focused on the most profitable products and services, or is it preoccupied with peripheral issues?
- What are the least profitable parts of the organisation, and how will these be improved?
- Are market and customer decisions focused on improving profitability? Too often the emphasis is put on such objectives as increasing market share or sales, which may involve a reduction in margins and greater financial exposure.
- How efficiently is cash managed in your organisation? Do your strategic business decisions take account of cash considerations, such as the time value of money? Are you giving more credit than you are receiving?

Managing risk

- Where are the greatest areas of risk relating to the most significant strategic decisions?
- What are the potentially dislocating events that could inflict the greatest damage on your organisation? (The scenario planning techniques outlined in Chapter 6 are valuable for assessing this issue.)
- What level of risk is acceptable for the company to bear?
- What is the overall level of exposure to risk? Has this been assessed and is it being actively monitored?
- What are the risks inherent in the organisation's strategic decisions, and what is the organisation's ability to reduce the incidence and impact on the business?
- What are the costs and benefits of operating effective risk-management controls?
- Are the risks inherent in strategic decisions (such as acquiring a new business, developing a new product, or entering a new market) adequately understood?
- At what level in the organisation are the risks understood and actively managed? Do people fully realise the potential consequences of their actions, and are they equipped to understand, avoid, control or mitigate risk?
- What review procedures are in place to monitor risks?
- To what extent would the company be exposed if key staff left?
- If there have been major new developments in the organisation (such as a new management structure or reporting arrangements), are the new responsibilities understood and accepted?

- Are management information systems keeping pace with demands? In particular, are there persistent "black spots", priority areas where the system needs to be improved or overhauled?
- Do people in the organisation resent risk, or are they encouraged to view certain risks as opportunities?

12 Sales, marketing and brand management decisions

Sales and marketing have become increasingly important functions in business as product differentiation has become less clear, and prices have become more transparent, market conditions more volatile and customers more fickle and assertive. All this has made decision-making more complex. This chapter's main focus is on meeting customer needs profitably, building on techniques outlined in Chapter 9 with regard to:

- Pricing
- Market entry
- Selling
- Using the internet to boost sales
- Brand management
- Product positioning
- Building customer loyalty

Pricing

Issues affecting pricing

Economic forces. The economic influences on pricing include monopoly and the extent of competition. Antitrust legislation aims to stop abuses of market power by big companies and to prevent mergers or acquisitions that would create a monopoly. Supply and demand affect pricing, because generally when supply exceeds demand prices will fall. The converse is also true: when demand exceeds supply prices will rise. One sales technique is often to stimulate demand by creating a perception of scarcity. Linked to this concept is price elasticity of demand, which highlights how the volume of demand is influenced by changes in price.

Market issues. Customer perceptions and behaviour – what the customer wants and expects – are among the biggest influences on pricing. Successful pricing is based on a clear understanding of the needs and nature of the target market. The culture of the market affects pricing decisions. If there is an acceptance of a particular type of pricing structure or approach, strategies will often follow this. The maturity of the market is also important. If the market is mature with few new customers, pricing decisions should focus on taking customers from competitors as well as retaining market share. But if the market is new and growing, the aim is to build and gain market share as rapidly as possible. These two approaches may or may not lead to the same result. Lastly, if the market is in decline, prices may need to be cut simply to compete for a dwindling number of customers.

Competitive issues. The competitiveness of the market affects pricing decisions. Where few direct competitors exist there may be a greater degree of latitude for pricing decisions. The nature of the competition also has an influence, as some competitors may be vulnerable to lower prices, chiefly if their costs prevent them lowering prices any further. Other competitors may be open to claims of poor value or quality. In this case, a higher price accompanied by appropriate advertising could reinforce perceptions of premium value and quality. An important rule is to target one competitor or a group of competitors, attacking them with the most appropriate pricing strategy.

Product issues. A product's costs are fundamentally significant when setting prices. It may make sense for products to be sold at a loss to establish market share or drive out competitors – although attention must be paid to any laws on predatory pricing. In any event, break-even analysis is a valuable method to use in setting prices (see Chapter 11). Lastly, and frequently of greatest significance, are the product's benefits and the value it provides for customers, although this must be closely related to other factors such as costs and competing products.

Pricing strategies

- **Loss leading** is a risky approach that involves selling a product at less than its cost in order to remove competitors or establish market share. It can be dangerous if the product becomes trapped with a low price.
- **Penetration pricing** combines a low, competitive price with aggressive sales techniques to penetrate the market and rapidly gain market share. It often works best when entering highly competitive markets.
- **Price differentiation** is an approach that charges variable prices for the same product in different markets, according to what customers are willing to pay.

- **Milking,** or charging a premium price for high-quality versions of an existing product, is a technique that works best when selling in an affluent market.
- **Target pricing** is one of the most common approaches where businesses target the level of profits that they wish to generate, estimate sales volumes at a specific price and then confirm that price. It relies on accurate estimates of sales volumes and generally ignores competitors' actions.
- **Average cost pricing** is similar to target pricing. Total costs and the desired profit margin are calculated and then divided by anticipated total sales. This is one of the most popular approaches to pricing. However, it too relies on accurate estimates of sales, as well as cost stability.
- **Marginal cost pricing** is also popular and is based on the extra cost of supplying one more item (for example, a printing company may quote a run-on price for extra copies).
- **Variable pricing** is an extreme measure that results in prices being reduced to stimulate business or raised to slow demand. The problems lie in explaining to customers why prices are fluctuating when the product is unchanged.
- **Customary pricing** involves charging the same price but reducing the specification of the product (for example, making the product smaller). Customers can find it misleading and resent a reduction in value.
- **Barrier pricing** is when prices are reduced, usually temporarily, to deter or remove competitors. It is an aggressive approach similar to loss leading, requiring both the will and the money to support it over time. It is most frequently seen in highly competitive markets, including consumer retailing.

Deciding the right price

It is good practice to do the following when deciding prices:

- **Calculate costs.** This involves checking all the direct costs of sales (and ideally attributing overhead costs as well) and understanding on what basis the costs are calculated.
- **Assess sales volumes and the firm's competitive strength.** Having understood the product's cost structure, it is helpful to estimate the likely volume of sales across a range of possible prices. This requires taking into account several factors: customer

needs, market maturity, sales techniques, the culture of the market and any expectations that may exist, the firm's overall strategy and ability to sustain the price, and the product portfolio.

◪ **Select the most appropriate pricing strategy.** Once the issues above have been addressed the pricing strategy can be decided. It may be desirable to follow prevailing pricing trends, or to take a different approach, actively competing on price. It is worth noting that price innovations can be achieved in various ways: for example, by altering factors linked to pricing, such as the size of a product or payment terms.

◪ **Review the pricing decision.** To ensure that pricing decisions are realistic you should consider:
  – how customers will perceive the price;
  – whether there are any issues of timing or seasonality affecting the price;
  – how easily the price can be sustained (once set, a price strategy needs to be consistently held, or confusion or resentment among customers may result);
  – the overall competitive situation and the likely response of competitors;
  – how the pricing decision relates to other areas of business strategy, including brand management, product profile and the future development of the business.

Market entry decisions

Decisions to enter new markets are notoriously hazardous. Being first into a market can give a firm first-mover advantage, enabling it to entrench itself and making it much harder for new competitors to succeed. There are several notable examples of firms that have achieved this position, but perhaps the best known is how Microsoft came to dominate the computer software market. Although it can be claimed that Microsoft was not, strictly speaking, the first into the market, this is to miss the point. It came to a market early, benefited massively from barriers to entry and gained economies of scale, and became one of the fastest-growing and wealthiest businesses in the world. However, the history of virtually every industry is littered with tales of disaster and lengthy lists of decisions that failed. Late entry into a market is not necessarily a problem if it means that mistakes are avoided and a better product is introduced. However, conventional wisdom says that the late entrant will be fighting more experienced businesses, which already possess the advantages of market share, such as an established brand reputation, customer base and cash flow.

Time for a change: Swatch's market entry

In the 1980s, the Swiss watch industry was at a crossroads. For many years, it had enjoyed a reputation for premium quality but it had been surrendering the popular, low-cost end of the market to Japanese companies. These were using their enviable reputation for technology, engineering and reliable low-cost production gained in other products (from cars to domestic appliances) and were squeezing the Swiss watch industry into an ever-diminishing niche at the top end of the market. (Interestingly, technology was causing this end of the market to shrink, as customers were buying Swiss watches that lasted for life and could even be passed on as heirlooms.) The Swiss, who had been market leaders for as long as anyone could remember, now found their expertise was counting against them: they were perceived as being out of touch and outmoded in the age of mass quartz crystal chronometers.

With an aggressive and imaginative campaign the Swiss moved to retake the industry that they had dominated for so long. Swatch launched a range of stylish watches aimed at a youthful mass market. Its comprehensive and sophisticated campaign involved massive media advertising, promotions and sponsorship events, and caught the public imagination. Its styling has since been applied to other industries. For example, when Daimler entered the market for urban runabout cars, it collaborated with Swatch, developing the Smart car.

Swatch has been successful and, unusually for a single company, has helped to redefine the market. For example, there are now watches for sports use, leisurewear and executives as well as traditional styles. Among the reasons for Swatch's success was a willingness to throw away the rulebook, understand the changing market and attempt to lead it. If the company had described its plans and produced prototypes ahead of launch it might have been ridiculed, but by understanding who it was targeting – younger, sporty people looking for style and reliability – and aggressively marketing the concept, it achieved one of the world's most successful market entries.

Factors affecting market entry

Market research and market sensing (discussed in Chapter 9) are important in providing an in-depth awareness of the market and informing issues relating to product development, pricing, marketing channels and sales techniques. Getting the product offer right is also essential. This means ensuring that the whole package, from product attributes and benefits to packaging, pricing and intangibles such as reliability and service, is based on an understanding of market conditions, customer needs and competitiveness. Sales forecasting tests the viability of the venture and can be used to check that there is an ability to meet demand. The most effective advertising and other promotional methods should be researched and developed to ensure that coverage of the target market is appropriate and cost-effective. Plans may also include developing new or extending existing sales channels.

Choosing a market position

There are generally perceived to be three market entry positions for any business:

- First mover (or pioneer)
- Early adopter (or second/third mover)
- Follower

It is generally assumed, incorrectly, that first mover and market leader are synonymous and that success requires early and massive domination of the market. All three market positions have advantages and disadvantages, and deciding early on the market position for a product or firm enables greater control and insight into future decisions.

1 **First movers.** First movers can define the product offer, set standards and, most valuably, gain market share and brand awareness. Yet there are significant difficulties and risks in being a first mover. The time and energy building market share may divert attention and resources from other parts of the business. And, because there are no previous entrants from whose experience you can learn, it is easier to make mistakes. First movers that have succeeded (such as Dell and Microsoft) have done so by, among other things, listening to customers, swiftly building and entrenching market share, and constantly driving innovations so that there is a stream of new products entering the market, ensuring that they do not get left behind. These things are hardly revolutionary, proving that there is no secret formula for success, just a constant desire to succeed.

2 **Early adopters.** Early adopters can either select profitable or promising market segments, or mimic the first mover's offering but add additional features to defeat it. The advantage is that early adopters can learn from the first mover (from its mistakes or success) and guarantee that their new approach moves the market on. The problem is that early adopters will inevitably be compared with the first mover, and every aspect of their offering and its relative strengths and weaknesses will be scrutinised. They also need to attack an entrenched market position and attract customers that may well be satisfied with the first mover. Furthermore, the margins are unlikely to be the same for early adopters as new market entrants usually create price pressures and a squeeze on margins.

What is needed is a clear focus on markets, customers and profits. The obvious approach is to target those areas where the first mover is weak or where it is not being responsive to the market. The second approach is to differentiate the early adopter from the first mover, perhaps by delivering a message that attacks the market leader or emphasises a vital source of competitive advantage. Early adopters need to know their strengths and their sources of competitive advantage, in respect of not only the first mover but also other potential market entrants, and then emphasise these. Early adopters can succeed by focusing on improving quality and reducing prices, which can be achieved by establishing efficient processes, value chains and supplier relations. This is also important when fighting the inevitable price war.

3 **Followers.** This group has the benefit of enjoying the clearest view of the market. Followers are able to analyse trends and best practices, which can help them discern business opportunities. The problems are that there is often a herd of followers stampeding into a market (if there is not then that is at least as worrying) and it may be difficult to find a sufficiently distinctive product offering. The most effective approach is to meet the needs of specific, tightly defined market segments and not to deviate from that market. Also important is the need to exploit cost advantages or economies of scale, possibly by buying a business that is already in the market.

Of course, once the market has been entered successfully the business must sustain its market focus and be able to constantly develop sources of competitive advantage.

Deciding to enter new markets

Many of the decisions relevant to entering new markets are also perti-nent to expanding within existing markets. The things to consider include market trends and opportunities, innovations, product benefits, pricing, the marketing mix, suppliers and, of course, competitors.

Consider market issues. Understanding the market means, above all, building a detailed knowledge of customers' needs and wants, as well as what they do not want. It is also essential to develop an appreciation of customer expectations, particularly in terms of quality, price, customer service and the sales process. Knowing who will buy and why are fun-damental questions. How, where and when they currently purchase and would like to purchase are also significant. The second thing to con-sider is competitors' strengths and weaknesses, but as these are likely to be past or present, it is also worth thinking about likely reactions to new entrants into the market. Lastly, it is important to understand whether the market is growing or shrinking.

Innovate. A valuable approach when entering new markets is to chal-lenge existing practices, so as to provide a better service and serve cus-tomers in a way that delivers (and ideally exceeds) their expectations. This requires skills of creativity and innovation, a talent for spotting opportunities and the ability to re-evaluate the way the business oper-ates. Questions to ask include:

- Why are things done the way they are?
- What would happen if they were approached differently, and what would be the implications of an innovative approach (for example, what would it mean for cash flow, production costs, sales volumes, pricing and brand reputation)?
- How will the position in the market be sustained and grown?
- Are there practices from other industries that could be emulated?

Focus on the product. Getting the product right before launch is often where most effort is spent, but developing a long-term strategy and direction for the product is important as well. Things to consider include how to make the product desirable with popular, distinctive (if not unique) benefits, deciding which product features to emphasise and planning future enhancements early.

Develop a pricing strategy. Getting the pricing strategy right depends on a number of things, including the competitive situation, product costs, product benefits and the nature of the market (see pricing decisions above).

Develop a sales plan. When entering new markets, it is useful to focus marketing efforts on quickly developing resources, including tangible factors such as cash, sales volumes and customers, and intangibles such as profile and brand reputation.[1] Things that can help establish firms in new markets include the following:

- Direct selling and key account management enable the largest potential customers to be targeted.
- Public relations activities raise awareness of the product, its principal features and benefits, as well as where to buy it.
- Internet selling is a low-cost technique with instant, widespread accessibility and the ability to provide targeted, detailed information at low cost.
- Database and direct-mail marketing enables potential customers to receive tailored information.
- Media advertising (magazines, newspapers, radio and television), although expensive, provides mass coverage.
- Trade fairs offer direct contact with current and potential customers and a venue to launch products that will reach opinion-formers (such as journalists).
- Special-offer promotions and samples are an eye-catching way of introducing new products, and they often work well for new and unknown entrants into a market.

Securing supply. Supply issues should be addressed before launching new products to ensure that quality standards and costs can be maintained, and that there is sufficient capacity to meet demand.

Extending activities with strategic partnerships and alliances. Alliances are an extremely effective way of testing a new market or establishing a new product in an existing market. They can be attractive when entering specialist or distant markets, for example in reaching little-known export markets. Partnerships may include distribution and agency agreements, licensing agreements, franchising or joint ventures.

Other things to consider when deciding how to enter a market include the speed and timing of entry, as the time required to become established varies considerably with each entry method. Profitability and level of risk, including such matters as the percentage taken by agents, distributors or other intermediaries, are important. Trade and economic issues, including tariffs, stability and infrastructure, and political issues, such as legal restraints on ownership or business activities, may also be decisive in determining the method of market entry.

The strategic importance of the market and its potential are significant in the choice of entry method. If the market is seen as having substantial growth potential and value, this would suggest a larger and more direct presence in order to exercise greater control. The availability, cost and skills of staff required in the new market may be relevant, as may the level of experience that the organisation possesses. The expertise and finance needed to implement the strategy will also influence the decision on how, where and when to enter new markets.

Selling decisions

Sales decisions are tough and unforgiving, as one wrong move can easily hand the initiative to competitors. Moreover, customers' perceptions, once formed, can be difficult to alter. Decisions should be informed by an understanding of and feel for how customers will react to a proposition, a commitment to service and a focus on profitability. It is often difficult to apply these principles, but there are several useful ways to keep sales decisions on track:

- View the situation from another perspective, ideally the customer's.
- Prepare a plan of action, an approach that will deliver success.
- Avoid basing decisions about customers on assumptions. Sustaining a productive dialogue with customers is more beneficial, giving greater insights of a higher quality.
- Share information and insights about customers throughout the organisation as this helps to co-ordinate activities and decisions. After all, success is much more likely if decisions are based on the same information and perceptions. Discussions with colleagues and others involved in important decisions (such as agents) can also be invaluable in ensuring success.
- Highlight the product's benefits, not simply its features, and highlight where it compares favourably with competitors' products.

- Consider cross-selling other products to existing customers and focus on increasing the value derived from individual clients. Discounts and special offers need not be offered to everyone; they are most effective when targeted at specific clients or groups of customers.
- Build customers' loyalty to your business and respect for your brand. If there is something about your business that appeals to customers, then they will be much easier to keep and sell to repeatedly. To achieve this, consider, as far as possible, what matters to each customer and bind all customers to the product through initiatives such as loyalty schemes.
- Consider using a range of incentives to close the deal, such as discounts or easier payment terms. But always be confident that when the deal is closed payment will actually be made on the terms agreed.
- Compete by developing uniqueness: either unique insights into customer needs that competitors do not possess, or innovative features in the product or sales process that are distinctive and popular, or both.
- Act quickly and decisively to impress or reassure customers. Hesitation, for whatever reason, may be interpreted as a lack of concern.
- Manage and update information systems so that they serve customers in all of these ways, ensuring a supportive approach.

Dell sell well: Dell Computer's sales techniques

In 1988, Dell Computer started competing aggressively with IBM and Compaq, the market leaders. Dell's strategy was to provide good-quality personal computers at low (but not the lowest) price, backed up with friendly and reliable after-sales service. But the key to Dell's success was that it carefully targeted its product by getting to know its customers. Large amounts of advertising were placed in new and, at the time, unfashionable magazines that were read by computer experts, raising Dell's profile with this significant group. At the same time, the company used direct-response advertising: in order to get the Dell product catalogue, customers had to either complete a detailed response card or call a toll-free number where they were asked the same questions. Dell's phone representatives were highly skilled, trained both to ask questions and to listen to customers, recording details of their preferences and requirements and then acting on them. Potential customers, flattered by the attention they received, responded in droves, enabling Dell to build an enormous database of useful information. This was then used to help customers, by tailoring products and services to individuals in a way that they understood and appreciated.

Using the internet to boost sales

Using the internet to sell has many advantages, and not simply the obvious one of connecting with more customers across a wide spectrum. However, the internet is also a source of strong, hidden undercurrents that can blow plans off course or drown them in technology. The internet reduces sales costs, broadens customer reach and has the potential to increase sales and market share. It has also fundamentally changed such industries as travel and bookselling. But whatever sector you are in, internet activities need to be integrated into the whole business.

Increasing sales

The internet enables sales to be made everywhere, all the time, which means that the business is available round the clock to sell and communicate with customers, constantly adding value. The goal is often to make an organisation the most accessible and the easiest to do business with. Surveys have suggested that as much as 75% of internet shopping carts are abandoned, leaving most transactions uncompleted. The challenge is therefore to encourage users to complete their purchases, not only with a compelling offer but also by guiding them through the sales process, providing customer-focused support and accurate information at every step. Increasing average order size is another potential benefit of the internet. This can be done by using the data from online transactions for cross-selling.

The internet can also be used to sell additional products, either add-ons or new product lines. The customer data collected can be segmented and then related to each individual customer's needs.

Reducing sales costs and improving efficiency

The internet enables sales people to have the latest, most up-to-date information to promote sales. This might include product information, testimonials, details of special offers and customer or market intelligence. This information is particularly valuable when in-depth product information is needed, and it can be provided directly to distributors as well as the salesforce.

The internet allows products to be evaluated quickly and easily without assistance, which can be particularly valuable for complex products or rapidly evolving markets. As a result, product and technical experts can be used for greater value-added activities. Furthermore, if the sales system is effective, complex, customised price quotations can be prepared for customers, possibly without sales people intervening. This has various advantages: it provides an immediate response to customers' enquiries, reduces the lead time for sales, ensures accurate hand-over of order details, and saves time and effort in taking and transmitting orders. In effect, everything is done better, more quickly and more cost-effectively. It also provides accuracy, another hidden benefit of the internet. This not only increases speed but also leads to great reductions in waste. Furthermore, depending on the industry and product, it can lead to reductions in inventory costs as products are made to order.

Building customer loyalty online

The internet makes it easier to achieve three key elements of customer loyalty: making it easy for customers to do business with you, satisfying your customers and ensuring that they come back. Furthermore, this can be accomplished at a fraction of the normal cost and, by building greater customer loyalty, sales costs are often reduced. There are several factors in building customer loyalty online.

- Customers will come back to a website if they feel comfortable and believe it is relevant to them, but more needs to be done to develop customer loyalty. Customers must feel that the website is simple, helpful and intuitive; in other words, it must be easy to use.
- The website must be responsive, understanding what customers want without marching them along a predetermined course. (This can be bad enough when a sales person does it; when a computer steers you in an unwanted direction it is particularly annoying.)
- The information should be accurate as well as immediate. Customers should be offered the chance to question or change choices before confirming details without worrying that the service will be incorrect.
- The website should be valuable, offering an element of service

that is unique and cannot be found elsewhere, with options that are likely to suit the target customer.

If an organisation can include all this in its website, the likelihood is that returned shipments, adjustments to orders and dissatisfied customers will decrease, combining cost reduction with an increase in customer loyalty.

Techniques to boost internet sales
Seven decisions can help to drive sales online:

- Generate participation, ownership and commitment within the whole company and among senior managers in particular, so that a co-ordinated, cross-functional approach is taken that increases value for the customer and reduces costs for the business.
- Ensure that the online sales strategy is all-embracing, enhancing existing activities and learning from past experience.
- Simplify the customer's experience so that the sales process is streamlined, with barriers to purchasing removed.
- Ensure that the website is sticky and compelling. You want customers to remain at the site when they arrive, and to return frequently.
- Focus on flexibility and efficient personalisation so customers are able to buy exactly what they want, how they want it.
- Avoid duplication and past mistakes; for example, avoid a complicated, high-cost solution when an effective, low-cost alternative is available.
- Prepare internally for the changes that an internet sales strategy will deliver so that the company avoids investing too much, too little, too late or too soon.

The best online sales decisions blend past experience and existing resources with the dynamism and invention of the internet. One useful principle is to use the flexibility of the internet, effectively testing new decisions and ideas. The technology and culture of the internet enable one approach to be tested for a short period before making improvements.

Ten things determine the success of online business activities, some or all of which are useful to consider when deciding how to develop online sales:

- Content
- Communication
- Customer care
- Community and culture
- Convenience and ease
- Connectivity (connecting with other sites as well as with users)
- Cost and profitability
- Customisation
- Capability (dynamic, responsive and flexible)
- Competitiveness

Each of these exerts a significant influence on the success of online activities. Some are more important than others, depending on the organisation's stage of development, brand strength and competitive position. Some are always important, such as capability and convenience, whereas others can assume a greater significance at a particular time (competitiveness, although always in the background, may assume a sudden and striking relevance).

Wired or tired: online decisions

In 1996, General Electric (GE) pioneered the use of an extranet (a closed network for use by people external to the organisation) in its lighting division to develop effective business-to-business relationships. The lighting division established a global network, linking with suppliers worldwide, to enable the company to complete its purchasing transactions more quickly. A feature of the extranet, known as the trade processing network (TPN), allowed GE's many international suppliers to download GE product specifications and communicate with the company via a secure, encrypted software link over the internet. The benefits of this approach for the lighting division were swift and significant: the cycle time in the purchasing process was reduced, enabling more efficient production and inventory management. GE suppliers continued to become an integrated part of a global community. Furthermore, TPN was employed in seven other GE business divisions as well as being licensed to other manufacturers to use with their suppliers.

In contrast, a survey of websites in 2000 found that 40% of e-mail questions went unanswered. Only 16% of sites followed up with a marketing offer to customers that had purchased from them in the last 30 days, and of these, only 2% were personalised. Other surveys suggest that as many as 60% of people using the internet believe that giving out personal information is "generally unsafe". Many businesses now recognise the commercial importance of ensuring that their websites are safe and secure, and are seen to be so by their customers.[2]

Brand management decisions
The significance of brands
A brand is a design, name or identity that is given to a product or service in order to differentiate it from its competitors. Brands are likely to remain a potent force in the future, not least because, in an increasingly unclear and uncertain world, they help customers understand what they are buying or are being offered. If you buy a Rolls-Royce, for example, you expect certain brand values such as quality, reliability and prestige. Brands are complex assets, and like people they possess, to some degree, distinguishing features. One increasingly popular method of managing brands is to view them as having "personalities". The Rolls-Royce brand has a high-class, high-quality appeal throughout the world, and retailers such as Wal-Mart and K-Mart built their reputations on homely convenience and low price. It is this concept of brand personality that highlights their power.

The advantage of brands
Before considering decisions that can build and strengthen brands, it is helpful to understand what advantages they offer. The value of a brand lies in the understanding or trust of customers. This leads to the first advantage: pricing. A successful and established brand can command a price premium that exceeds any extra cost in terms of production and marketing, derived from the element of trust that a brand provides. Research in the UK has shown that in many cases consumers would be prepared to pay 30% more for a new product from a trusted brand than for an unnamed one. This is particularly true in the highly competitive food industry.

Distribution advantages are another benefit, as an established brand can ensure that manufacturers get the best distributors in terms of quantity and quality. This is because the distributors are more likely to be receptive to a new product from an established brand, in much the same way (and for similar reasons) as their consumers. This is particularly useful for new products. Again, this is because of the element of trust and reliability associated with brands.

The concept of brand identity or image is valuable as it reinforces the product's appeal. For example, the Rolls-Royce brand has a stately identity and is associated with the values of craftsmanship, tradition and prestige. Volvo has a different brand identity and set of associated values, including safety, functionality and family-orientation. These identities reinforce their appeal to their particular market segments. When markets decline, however, brand identity can become a handicap, linking the product to an unfashionable past.

This links with the next advantage: the ability of brands to build customer loyalty, again because of the trust and even affection that they can generate. Customer groups can identify preferred brands easily, becoming repeat purchasers. A classic example is the old adage "no one ever got fired for buying IBM". In this extreme case, even when consumers did not necessarily like the product, they still respected the brand.

Another advantage of brands is that businesses can launch profitable new products with a flying start by exploiting the popularity and strength of an established brand. Cherry Coke and Diet Coke are examples of this approach, where the strong, established Coca-Cola brand (probably one of the strongest commercial brands in history) underpinned the launch of these two new drinks. This reinforced the brand still further by attacking the competition, adding another dimension to the brand (innovation) and developing new markets (such as the diet soda market). There are two benefits: brands often make it easier to introduce new products by exploiting "brand equity"; and they provide opportunities to open up new market segments. For example, food manufacturers often exploit their position to create sub-brands of diet versions (such as an established yogurt manufacturer successfully launching a low-fat product).

Furthermore, a strong brand can enable the product to overflow from one market into another, allowing the brand to spread in popularity. This is particularly the case in industries that are affected to a greater or lesser degree by fashion. For example, the strength and popularity of coffee houses such as Starbucks grew during the 1990s, spreading from the American north-west to the whole of the country and then to Europe.

Brands can extend the life of a product, as by their nature they combine trust, respect, profile and marketing spend. This can often be used to inject new life into a stagnating product or even a whole industry. The example of Danish toymaker Lego producing toys linked with films is an example of this trend. Lastly, brands provide a valuable, market-oriented focus around which firms can organise themselves. The brand manager is often directly responsible for what the product offers as well as how it appears to the customer.

Brand-building decisions

Building a brand is complex, expensive and time-consuming. Sometimes it is seen as a natural by-product of building a successful business, and sometimes it is specifically targeted as a priority in its own right. Either way, there are several decisions upon which the successful development of a brand depends.

1 **Decide the brand's purpose.** The greatest priority is deciding how the brand will be used. For example, is it to provide reassurance, to enable a premium price to be charged or to create a desire to buy? There are other things to consider. What benefits can the brand offer customers? These may be emotional or rational. How reliable and trustworthy is the brand? Is it credible in the eyes of the customer? For established brands the market value needs to be assessed. Is it increasing or declining, and what is affecting its success?

2 **Emphasise the brand's values.** The next priority is to understand what the brand means to customers, or what it is intended to mean, and then to find ways to deepen this appeal. This can be achieved by considering all aspects of the brand. For example, to whom does it appeal? Is the tone of voice commensurate with the brand values, target market and any existing perceptions? If you were to describe the brand as an entity, what would you choose and why?

3 **Use the brand.** Understanding how the brand differentiates a product from its competitors is important in deciding which attributes to emphasise and how to target competitors. This can be explored by considering what makes the brand different. What makes it exceptional? How special is the brand and how easily could it be replicated? Ideally, there should be sufficient barriers to replication to ensure that the brand remains strong and distinctive. An audit of the brand will be helpful in determining how strong and credible it appears to customers and will give some insight into the extent to which the brand can be stretched into new markets, and the values that could enable (or disable) this from happening. Also to be considered is whether there is sufficient investment in the brand and how it can be strengthened.

Product positioning decisions

The concept of positioning relates to how a product is perceived by customers relative to its competitors. It originated in the advertising industry as a way of identifying those attributes of a product that should be placed in the buyer's consciousness. For example, a product may be positioned as inexpensive, innovative, old fashioned, prestigious, high quality or any of a multitude of other attributes. Positioning influences attitudes to and perceptions of a product or company brand, rather than changing the product itself. The value of positioning decisions is that they increase awareness of a company's or product's capabilities. Positioning can refresh or reinforce an existing brand or explain a specific concept. It links closely with such things as brand management, competitive strategy, pricing, segmentation and market entry strategies.

Avoiding blood on the carpet: repositioning at Dupont

When Dupont, an industrial conglomerate, realised that it was not selling enough fibres for use in the carpeting industry, it decided to look at the whole value chain: carpet manufacturers, wholesalers, distributors (retailers) and customers. It found that many customers preferred tiles or wooden floors for ease of maintenance and durability, but also because of unsatisfactory experiences with carpet retailers. Reasons for their dissatisfaction included inconvenient locations, unimpressive ranges, lack of samples, unreliable delivery and poor fitting.

Dupont changed its division from carpet fibre to flooring systems and started to think more of the decorative and fashion features of carpets, rather than just the functional ones (robustness, stain resistance, durability, noise and heat insulation). Consequently, it developed information for the whole value chain, including new information and advertising for customers on how to buy and maintain carpeting, and the Dupont hotline for retailers, providing answers for consumer questions. Dupont's expertise on products, selling and understanding consumers was also available to retailers on video, and the company provided information on market trends for carpet manufacturers, wholesalers and retailers.

Deciding where to position a product

Positioning depends first on finding a niche or part of the market where there is space to establish a profitable position. To discover whether one exists requires an understanding of the trends and factors influencing the market.

How best to focus on the customer is another important decision. How will potential customers react to the message or offer? Or, to put it another way, what message will have the greatest impact on the customer?

With positioning decisions, timing is important. First movers have a head start and can get to know the market in detail and build a strong customer-base, ideally establishing a rapport with customers. Brands that are not the first mover should endeavour to launch when the market leader is weak or quiet, or both.

Thought needs to be given to how one avoids head-on confrontation with the market leader, the brand with the most to lose. The market leader can be expected to react strongly against newcomers with the aim of crushing them before they have a chance to get established. The brand that is attacking the market leader therefore needs a valuable, attention-grabbing benefit or distinguishing feature, and the ability to convey its message convincingly.

Once a position has been taken, the decisions that follow should ensure that it is consistently defended. Consistency is essential: positioning means striving for leadership in one particular area. Another important decision is therefore the choice of a powerful and simple message. For example, Volkswagen launched the Beetle in the United States with the slogan "Small is Beautiful" and for many years Mars bars purported to help you "Work, Rest and Play" (particularly if eaten every day). But you must know how the message will be received. Often the best way to establish a position is to associate with something that may already be in people's minds. An example is customers' desire for value, highlighted by low-cost airlines, such as easyJet, Ryanair and South-West Airlines, which emphasise their no-frills service and low prices.

Building customer loyalty

One popular method of building repeat business is through customer loyalty schemes. Their inventiveness can be surprising, providing insights into the brand values of the company as well as the threat that they pose to competitors. Virgin Atlantic, for example, has an ingenious way of using such schemes: to reduce the time it takes to get new customers, it offers privileges to people involved in competitors' loyalty schemes. For a while, Virgin offered a free companion ticket to any British Airways frequent flyer who had accumulated 10,000 miles.

This had the added advantage of reinforcing perceptions of the Virgin brand as being dynamic and flexible, if somewhat bold and outrageous.

The road to success: helping customers buy

In the early 1990s, Ryder, the largest truck-leasing company in the world, suffered a steady decline in sales as competitors eroded its business. The company's main response was to use information more effectively to benefit customers. Its approach had three elements:

- **To help customers buy.** Ryder made it as easy as possible for customers to buy its services. For example, it produced a brochure explaining why customers should buy its damage insurance, and another offering other supplies and accessories. It also recognised that customers would want to make comparisons among competitors (they were doing this anyway), so it produced a truck comparison chart, highlighting its competitiveness and reassuring potential customers.
- **To help customers use the service.** Ryder provided a free guide to moving, *The Mover's Advantage*, in Spanish and English, to every current and potential customer. It understood why customers used its trucks and saw the advantage in helping them.
- **To help customers adapt their usage.** As well as ensuring that each outlet displayed a strong commitment to customer service and corporate identity, Ryder offered new products and services from its outlets. This included information about the advantages of using Ryder's towing equipment and longer-term discount rates for returning customers.

The effect of these measures was monitored through customer-satisfaction surveys placed in each truck. As well as checking that customers were satisfied, the surveys also served to highlight Ryder's renewed commitment to service, enhancing future sales prospects. Other measures helped to establish credibility with customers and improved the image that the business projected. For example, testimonials were featured in marketing literature, and each outlet was inspected monthly rather than quarterly to ensure that literature, banners and signage were appealing. This approach turned Ryder's business round during a recession, returning the company to the number one position in its industry.

Because customer loyalty is accepted as being fundamentally important, its impact on profits is rarely examined. However, how customer loyalty decisions feed profitability can be assessed by:

- measuring the profitability of customers;
- developing a customer's lifetime value;
- targeting, attracting and retaining customers.

Measuring the profitability of customers

This will help to determine the structure, resources, direction and development of the sales effort, enabling the business to develop its activities. To achieve this, customer analysis should highlight profit per customer, identifying the best and least profitable customers. It is also important to understand the characteristics of the most profitable customers, both to continue to meet their needs and to support tailored marketing campaigns that will attract the right customers.

Customer profitability can be measured by analysing two things: customer revenue and customer costs, including defection and retention costs. Some of the most important are listed in Table 12.1.

Identifying the most and least profitable customers enables current and future initiatives to be targeted at the most profitable customers. It may also allow the business to find ways of reducing the costs of doing business with the least profitable customers.

Developing a customer's lifetime value

The concept of customer lifetime value is not new, but it is worth considering how customer loyalty and repeat business develop profitability. Most obviously, the longer customers stay with the business the more they will spend over time. This is profitable because having sold once, there is likely to be less need to market or sell to them to attract them back; the only requirement is to focus on the quality of the value proposition. Loyal customers also provide a base on which to build market share, which in turn provides a platform from which to develop new commercial opportunities. For example, it can be used to attract advertisers or to entrench the business's position in the market.

Repeat business often leads to referral revenue. If customers are pleased with the service they will tell others, and they can be offered incentives to do so. Satisfied customers may be receptive to new products as well as (or instead of) their original purchase. By clearly understanding what the customer wants, you can cross-sell other products.

Table 12.1 **Measuring customers' profitability**

Factors affecting customer revenue	Factors affecting customer costs
Revenue per customer	Cost per customer (cost of sale as well as total cost per customer)
Number of orders per customer	Cost per order
Referrals from customers	Cost of retaining customers (cost of loyalty programmes and special offers)
Reasons for not purchasing (or going to a competitor)	Cost of acquiring a new customer
Future needs and likely volume and value of purchases	Likely (or target) growth and future cost implications
Note: understand the reasons for purchasing, what product or service attributes the customer values most	Note: assess the factors affecting cost and how these can be managed, monitored and controlled

Moreover, if these new products do not exist, you can have the confidence to develop them.

Another way in which customer loyalty drives profitability is through the ability to increase prices to loyal customers, because, of all the possible purchasers, they are the ones best placed to understand the value of your products. Loyal customers do not typically require discounts or product add-ons to stay with you. If they are happy with the product or service they are buying and if it is competitive, they will not normally be tempted away. Clearly, this depends on variables such as the nature of the market, but there is an element of inertia in most markets. Loyal customers can also be used to help with market testing of new products. This not only saves money in testing through other means, but it is also often much more effective.

Targeting, attracting and retaining customers

1 **Mass personalisation.** It was during the 1950s and 1960s that marketing first came to real prominence. In the 1970s, the focus shifted to techniques for mass marketing within an industry, highlighting techniques for reaching customers on a broad scale. In the 1980s and throughout the 1990s, the focus moved on to market segmentation, improving the

way that customers in specific markets were identified and reached. Now the focus has narrowed even further, with technology offering businesses the opportunity for mass personalisation. This is the ability to reach individual customers – targeting the right customers and then fulfilling their market needs – on a massive scale.

2 **Understand which customers to attract, and how.** Once a profile of potential customers has been drawn up and their needs and wants identified, it is then possible to:

- ◪ ensure that their needs are met and that the value proposition is compelling enough to sustain their interest;
- ◪ decide how best to appeal to this audience, considering everything from tone of voice to frequency of contact;
- ◪ decide how to engage the target market – when to ask for input, whether to offer discounts and generally how to ensure that the product offer is sufficiently attractive;
- ◪ decide how to capture details of enquirers so that they can be contacted later.

This list is by no means exhaustive. The trick is to start focusing on the target customers and ways of attracting them. It is also worth considering two other things. First, it is important to understand not only which customers to attract, but also which ones you definitely do not want to lose. Second, remember that the customer who makes the purchase may not be the person who decides to make the purchase or the end user, as is often the case with purchases by businesses.

Riding high: Harley-Davidson's customer loyalty programme

From its beginnings in Milwaukee in 1909, Harley-Davidson has enjoyed a long history as America's foremost motorbike manufacturer. However, by the early 1980s its reputation and business were in serious trouble following a sustained onslaught from affordable, high-quality Japanese machines produced by companies such as Honda and Kawasaki. Following a management buy-out, Harley-Davidson tackled its product-quality problems using the techniques of W. Edwards Deming (ironically, an American whose quality methods transformed Japanese manufacturing). The next challenge was to win back and maintain market share. This the company achieved, once again becoming America's leading motorbike manufacturer, with an amazing 90% of Harley-Davidson customers staying loyal to the company.

Harley-Davidson used several methods to bond with its customers, and each one combines knowledge of individual customer's needs with a cleverly judged appeal to their emotions. For example, the company's managers regularly meet customers at rallies, where new models can be sampled with free demonstration rides. Advertising reinforces the image and perception of owning a Harley, persuading existing customers to stay loyal as much as attracting new ones. The Harley Owner's Group (HOG) activities are central to binding customers to the company, and rather than providing trite or cheap benefits Harley devotes considerable resources to ensuring that its customers receive benefits that they value. Membership of HOG is free for the first year for new Harley owners and then a membership fee of approximately $40 is payable; over two-thirds of customers renew. It might seem easy to sell a product as exciting and appealing as a motorbike, but Harley-Davidson also manages to persuade tens of thousands of customers to keep on buying its machines, as well as paying to attend rallies where they enjoy themselves, make friends and provide valuable customer feedback. Some even tattoo themselves with the name of the company. How many businesses achieve that?

3 Focus on customers generating the most profit growth

This means identifying customers with the greatest profit potential, rather than the ones who are most profitable now. Businesses often try to be all things to all people, disregarding the need to retain a focus on the most profitable parts of the market. Customer loyalty may be important, but if the cost of ensuring a customer's loyalty outweighs the benefits and revenue of that customer, why bother? Maintaining market share for its own sake is often an unwise approach. If a customer cannot be retained without losing money, then it is better to lose that customer and focus on those that will help improve profitability.

4 Understand what builds customer loyalty and what destroys it

Table 12.2 lists some dos and don'ts when building customer loyalty.

Ways to build customer loyalty

If you build trust and rapport with customers by listening to, understanding and helping them, they are more likely to be loyal. And the more you are able to tailor information and special offer promotions to individual customers the more likely they are to remain loyal. The Holy

Table 12.2 Decisions that build or destroy customer loyalty

Do	Don't
Deliver customers a consistent (and ideally a "branded") experience each time they deal with your business	Overcomplicate the product offer; when selling, clarity works
Be clear about the value proposition: what you are offering customers	Change the offer too frequently
Provide incentives to return and reorder for new customers	Stay the same for too long
Reward loyalty for established customers	Avoid asking the customer or seeing the purchase from the customer's perspective
Be competitive: what seems like a good deal to you may not be enough to match your competitors in the eyes of your customers	Ignore problems and potential pitfalls: identify them early, resolve them or put contingency plans in place should they be needed
Make the customer's experience as easy and enjoyable as possible	Focus on internal divisions; instead, emphasise issues of greatest relevance and interest to customers
Reassure customers with a reliable service and product offer that delivers peace of mind	Target everyone; instead, focus on how to appeal to your most profitable customer groups
Continuously improve the process based on customer feedback	Fail to communicate, both internally and externally
Deliver reliability by working with partners and investing in the resources to benefit customers	Control customers; instead, allow them to feel in control

Grail of marketing has long been the ability to meet the needs of individual customers to drive revenue and profit; this is now easier to achieve, especially online.

Try to build on the initial purchase so that it is not simply a once-only transaction but provides an opportunity to make further offers that will be attractive to the customer.

Key questions

Sales, marketing and brand management decisions can be as difficult as they are important. Below are some of the issues that may need to be considered on a regular basis.

Pricing

- How elastic are product prices? Could prices be increased without reducing revenue?
- When is the next price rise planned? Could it happen sooner?
- Are forces driving down prices in your market? What are they and how can you counter them?
- Who fixes prices in your organisation? How do they do it and could the process be improved?
- Are discounts targeted at the right sectors, or are they needlessly eroding profitability?
- Could pricing be used more aggressively?

Market entry

- What are the barriers to entry in your market? How much of a barrier are they? Could you make it even harder for competitors to enter the market?
- When is the best time to enter or leave the market? Can action be taken to discourage and reduce the effectiveness of competitors entering?
- If you are planning to enter a new market, what makes your offer distinctive and likely to succeed?
- Are other firms entering the market? If not, why?

Selling

- Do people in your organisation view sales from the customers' perspective?
- How well do people in your organisation know each individual customer? Could more data be gathered and assessed?
- Do people in your organisation share information and insights about customers?
- Are product benefits (not simply product features) highlighted?
- Could you sell more to existing customers?
- Do people in your organisation act decisively and swiftly to reassure and impress customers?

Using the internet to boost sales
- ◪ Do you take a co-ordinated approach to selling online?
- ◪ Is buying online an easy and worthwhile experience for the customer? How could it be improved?
- ◪ Is the website attractive, practical and relevant, learning from the lessons of the early years of website design?
- ◪ Are you ready for the changes that may result from greater internet sales?

Brand management
- ◪ What is the purpose of the brand? What values does it need to emphasise to customers?
- ◪ How can the brand be used to greatest effect?
- ◪ Is sufficient attention given to building and publicising the brand?
- ◪ Is the brand used consistently?

Product positioning
- ◪ Is the product in the best part of the market, or is repositioning needed?
- ◪ What is the best way to appeal to customers? How should the product be sold?
- ◪ Avoiding a head-on confrontation with the market leader is often a wise course. Is this happening, or are you in danger of waking a sleeping giant?
- ◪ Is a simple, consistent and compelling message being used to sell the product?

Building customer loyalty
- ◪ Do you measure the profitability of customers?
- ◪ Are you targeting, attracting and retaining the most profitable customers?
- ◪ What plans are in place to keep customers loyal? Are they appealing to customers and difficult for competitors to copy?

13 Leadership

Good leadership and good decision-making go hand in hand. Effective leadership depends on an ability to know when to press ahead and when to change course, as well as the ability to show purpose and direction. This is essential when mobilising people, determining priorities and generating commitment.

This chapter outlines the role of leaders in ensuring that strategic decisions are effectively developed and implemented. It provides a guide to achieving this as well as a summary of the main ideas and themes behind such decision-making.

Decisive leadership

Effective decision-making depends on a collection of leadership skills that can be learnt and are often closely linked. These include the following:

- An ability to foster innovation and creativity and to exploit synergies between people, sometimes disparate and distant teams.
- The intelligence and courage to recognise and learn from mistakes.
- The perception and sensitivity to analyse competing options, and the ability to help others to find their solutions.
- Skills of delegation and empowerment so that decision-making can be devolved to others in the organisation with sufficient time or insight.
- The capacity to motivate people so that they are inspired to prevent or solve problems themselves, as well as proactively implementing decisions.
- An ability to focus others on the twin issues of serving customers and managing change.
- Skilled communication.
- The courage and ability to make critical decisions.

Fostering innovation and creativity

Many people have trouble in coming up with new ideas or solutions to a problem. The answer often lies in fostering innovation, by creating the right conditions to be innovative or simply to see the best way forward.

If this is to work and be sustainable, the climate for decision-making must be as positive, open and encouraging as possible. Linked with this is the need for people to feel valued. If they do not, there is a risk that they will be negative about the change, reactive rather than proactive. Or they may decide to leave.

One way of fostering innovation is to encourage employees to question the way things are done or decisions that have been made. Removing or minimising barriers (such as bureaucracy and hierarchy) can drive innovation, and so can an ability to exert mild pressure, perhaps by setting deadlines. Techniques that help spur creativity and innovation include brainstorming and mind mapping, as they help individuals to come up with ideas and to see patterns or organise information in such a way that patterns and ideas develop.

Encouraging innovation means listening to suggestions with an open mind.

> An expert problem-solver must be endowed with two
> incompatible qualities – a restless imagination and a patient
> pertinacity.
>
> Howard W. Eves, quoted in *Fermat's Last Theorem*[1]

This matters because people will support a decision and its implementation if they feel that they have been involved in the decision, and if it has been arrived at with intelligence and sensitivity. By listening to people's opinions and suggestions, and taking them into account, the final decision should, in theory at least, be better.

Learning from mistakes

As Daniel C. Dennett, a philosopher, explains:

> Making mistakes is the key to making progress ... Mistakes are
> not just golden opportunities for learning; they are, in an
> important sense, the only opportunity for learning something
> new ... Biological evolution proceeds by a grand, inexorable
> process of trial and error – and without the errors the trials
> wouldn't accomplish anything.[2]

Learning from mistakes also highlights another important aspect of decisive leadership: courage and the ability to stand alone. In the words of George Bernard Shaw:

> *The reasonable man adapts himself to the world: the*
> *unreasonable one persists in trying to adapt the world to*
> *himself. Therefore all progress depends on the unreasonable*
> *man.*

A natural tendency to evaluate the present or focus on the immediate decision should be tempered with a sense of perspective and the past. As discussed in Chapter 3, you need to avoid misinterpreting the lessons of the past or using events to justify current decisions but with a spurious logic. The anchoring, sunk-cost and confirming evidence traps are all behavioural flaws that rely on specific attitudes to past events. A genuine understanding of the past is crucial, but it needs to be related to what is happening in the present and kept in perspective. As Julian Barbour, a theoretical physicist, says:

> *The higher we climb, the more comprehensive the view. Each*
> *new vantage point yields a better understanding of the*
> *interconnection of things. What is more, gradual accumulation*
> *of understanding is punctuated by sudden and startling*
> *enlargements of the horizon, as when we reach the brow of a*
> *hill and see things never conceived of in the ascent. Once we*
> *have found our bearings in the new landscape, our path to the*
> *most recently attained summit is laid bare and takes its*
> *honourable place in the new world.*[3]

Scenario thinking (see Chapter 6), and in particular the notion of the strategic conversation described by Kees van der Heijden, enables us to build our knowledge and understanding of the past and present, making connections and creating original insights that inform our decisions.

Analysing competing options

A lack of sufficiently thorough analysis is common in decision-making. The natural tendency is for people to gravitate towards a particular option, often because of prejudice, fear (especially fear of change), a desire to avoid risk, laziness, or an over-reliance on instinct. Chapter 4 highlighted the importance of carefully assessing the situation, defining critical issues and specifying the decision. These are the first three stages of the rational decision-making process. Combining "hard" factors such as data, technology and information with "soft" factors of intuition, experience and creativity can test potential decisions. It is important to question assumptions and see things from another perspective (such as that of the customer or person most affected by the decision).

One way of appraising competing options is to look at the desired outcome and then see which option will achieve it. This simple approach is often complicated by the need to prioritise goals, reduce costs or minimise risk, and in selecting the best option usually involves trade-offs and compromise. Another approach is to establish criteria for the final decision – for example, it needs to work quickly, not be expensive, take a reasonable amount of time to organise and so forth – and then score each option against these components on a scale of 1–10. The highest-scoring option wins. With both approaches, you need to fully understand what each option requires, how it works and what it achieves.

Delegating

The success or failure of a decision frequently depends on the delegation process. Empowerment, which is discussed below, goes beyond the delegation of specific tasks. It involves granting a defined level of authority and responsibility within which someone makes their own decisions and implements them.

There are several stages in the delegation process.

- **Preparing to delegate.** Some preparation and planning are always needed, perhaps limited to gaining the approval of others or simply informing people. Priorities may also need to be considered. Most of all, you should be clear about the reasons for delegation and what it is meant to achieve. This requires a focus on results and having clear, precise objectives.
- **Matching person and task.** The person who is required to do the job must understand it and have the personal skills and competence to have a realistic chance of doing it successfully.
- **Discussing and agreeing objectives.** Targets, resources, review times and deadlines should be discussed with the delegatee and agreed. It may be necessary to formalise the process in writing in order to avoid, or at least minimise, any misunderstanding.
- **Providing resources and the appropriate level of authority.** When delegating work, it is imperative to provide the delegatee with the necessary resources as well as the authority to complete the task, and then to provide support when needed.
- **Monitoring progress.** Delegation of responsibility is not

abdication of responsibility. Monitoring does not mean interfering, distracting or undermining, but it does means checking progress at agreed times to verify that things are on track and to provide support.

▪ **Reviewing overall progress.** A final review provides a chance for both the delegator and the delegatee to learn. This is best achieved by reviewing outcomes against the original objectives.

Empowering people

Empowerment is defined by the UK Chartered Management Institute as follows:

> *Empowerment is a genuine opening up of the creative power of your people. It is based on the belief that employees' abilities are frequently underused and that given the chance and the responsibility, people want to make a positive contribution.*

Empowerment goes further than delegation and is a way of letting people exploit their potential more fully. In essence, it means letting individuals get on with their jobs, encouraging those people closest to the action to make their own decisions. It requires support, trust and a willingness to remove obstacles and bureaucracy, encouraging and enabling people to put their ideas for improvement into practice.

Empowering people to make decisions and then implement them requires leaders to:

▪ set a clear direction and ensure that people remain on course;
▪ encourage people to be innovative and use their initiative, usually within agreed boundaries;
▪ retain a full understanding of what is happening;
▪ create a positive, supportive and blame-free environment;
▪ offer support and clear the way for action without taking over from those doing the job;
▪ make decisions which others cannot, because of lack of time, information or knowledge;
▪ continuously assess performance and reward progress, supporting individual and team development;
▪ build trust through shared information and knowledge whenever possible.

Motivating people

For people to implement decisions successfully and to have the confidence to make decisions themselves, they must be motivated. In a team, the leader should understand exactly what motivates individual team members to act, what external influences are affecting them and what the leader's role is in the process. There are eight rules of motivation:

- Be motivated yourself, setting a clear example and driving progress forward.
- Understand what motivates people and choose people who themselves are highly motivated.
- Treat each person as an individual and avoid making assumptions about them.
- Set realistic and challenging targets.
- Remember that progress motivates, because it reinforces confidence.
- Create a motivating environment. How you do this depends on the task and the individual, but it might, for example, mean pressuring or stimulating people to act, or removing obstacles to action.
- Recognise success. This helps sustain momentum and contributes to continuing success.
- Provide fair rewards. They are a form of recognition and can encourage as well as develop trust and commitment.

A powerful vision also helps to motivate people. A comment by John F. Kennedy, a former American president, is a good example:

> We choose to go the moon in this decade and do the other
> things – not because they are easy, but because they are hard.
> Because that goal will serve to organise and measure the best
> of our abilities and skills, because that challenge is one that we
> are willing to accept, one we are unwilling to postpone, and
> one which we intend to win.

People respond best when they understand what they are doing and why they are doing it. An effective leader must have the ability to create and communicate a convincing and realistic vision that will sustain an organisation and its people through both good times and bad. Such a vision encapsulates a set of values that will guide decisions and action and build confidence, teamwork and consistency.

As well as being convincing and realistic, a vision should be powerful if it is to excite and inspire. It must also be easy to get across to everyone and it must be specific enough to be genuinely useful in decision-making. It must also be flexible enough to allow for individual initiative and changing conditions.

Serving customers and managing change

For a commercial enterprise, knowledge of its actual and potential customers informs a wide range of decisions. But markets and the customers that comprise them are constantly subject to change. Thus leaders need to understand where, how, when and why developments are occurring in order to ensure that the decisions they make are not wrong or undermined by changing circumstances. Several things make a difference:

- A clear vision promotes a shared sense of purpose, making it easier to act with flexibility, adapting to changing circumstances.
- It is important to ensure that bureaucracy does not constrain decisions or the need for action.
- People's skills should be developed so that they can meet the challenges created by developing circumstances.
- Confronting problems and their root causes early prevents frustration and preserves the momentum for change.

Communicating

All decisions should be explained to all who are affected by them so as to avoid misunderstandings. The explanation should highlight where the pitfalls and problems may lie as well as the benefits. There should be communication throughout the decision-making process in order to build and sustain support for the eventual decision and to make sure that those affected feel involved.

Handling critical decisions

Critical decisions are those that cannot afford to be wrong or to fail. They may be part, perhaps a vital one, of a larger process or a sudden crisis, or they may simply be in an area that is critically important. The 1962 Cuban missile crisis is an example. The Soviet Union was installing nuclear weapons in Cuba, 90 miles from mainland America, prompting a naval blockade of the island. The two superpowers were at a dangerous impasse. After a tense stand-off, President Kennedy received a message from Nikita Khrushchev, the Soviet leader, saying that the weapons would be removed. This was followed within hours by a second message saying that the withdrawal was conditional on America's removing nuclear weapons from bases in Turkey, which was unacceptable to the Americans. Kennedy decided to ignore the second message. He quickly wrote to Khrushchev accepting the withdrawal outlined in the first letter. Although Kennedy did not know it at the time, the second message had been sent first. One of the outcomes of this crisis was the establishment of a hotline, a direct telephone link between the leaders of the two countries, to ensure that such potentially disastrous misunderstandings were never repeated.

Because the very nature of critical decisions brings unusual pressure, those who have to take them may find the following techniques useful:

- **Balance detail with an overall view.** That is, pay constant attention to detail while keeping in mind the overall objective.
- **Trust your intuition.** When making critical decisions you must trust your judgment, accept responsibility and avoid any temptation to shy away from making the decision or to shift responsibility (see Chapter 4).
- **Stay committed.** It is always worth considering contingency measures and fallback positions, but it is important to remain committed to a decision. Critical decisions are often subject to in-depth analysis and criticism because they matter so much, and any wavering in commitment can quickly cause the decision and its implementation to unravel.
- **Avoid paralysis by analysis.** Avoid the mistake of endlessly analysing the options and never reaching a decision. When the risk factor is high, decisions can drift. Although it is perfectly acceptable, and even advisable, to take your time and analyse, consider and discuss, there comes a time to act and this point needs to be recognised by the leadership. There may be reasons to be risk averse, but fear of failure should not be one of them.
- **Assess all available options.** Take a broad view in selecting options. Considering the wider impact of a decision will help ensure that the right choice is made and implemented. Avoid tunnel vision and consider the effects of the decision on others. Understand the factors that influence how the decision will work in practice, and acknowledge expectations and the environment in which the decision is being made. The danger of paralysis by

analysis is outlined above, but the opposite is also hazardous: the belief that research is unnecessary or irrelevant, or that you don't have time for it.

◪ **Minimise risk.** Consider how the level of risk can be reduced, by increasing the likelihood of success but also by considering what can be done if things start going adrift. Developing the sensitivity and ability both to take risks when needed and reduce risks when required is difficult. There are several questions to ask when managing risk (see Chapter 11):
  - What might be the consequences of failure (worst case)?
  - What is the likelihood of failure?
  - What are the alternatives – and the consequences and likelihood of them failing?
  - How can the element of risk be minimised?

The aim must be to reduce both the likelihood and the consequences of failure. Most strategic decisions involve risk, and over time the riskiest option may be to play safe and do little, avoiding opportunities that have an element of uncertainty. Risk brings reward, and in the view of Harold Geneen, the former chairman of ITT:

> One of the primary, fundamental faults with American management is that over the years it has lost its zest for adventure, for taking risk, for doing something that no one has done before.

◪ **Base decisions on the best available information.** Decision-makers must be well informed if they are to make the right decision. As Geneen put it:

> I came to see that an objective view of the facts was one of the most important aspects of successful management. People go wrong most often when their decisions are based upon inadequate knowledge of the facts available.

It is tempting to dismiss some information as being obvious or irrelevant, rather than taking the time to build on it, constructing original insights.

◪ **Be practical.** Get back to first principles. Rather than getting mired in details, ask: "What are we trying to achieve?" This may seem trite, but it is often forgotten amid pressures and processes. Critical decisions can fail because although they seem logical in theory, in practice they are unworkable.

Seeing what's down the road: GM's Chinese investment

In 1997, General Motors signed a long-term joint-venture deal with a state-owned Chinese car manufacturer. The deal gave GM privileged access to the small but potentially large Chinese market for high-quality cars. However, after it was agreed, the Chinese made substantial cuts in tariffs on imported cars and spare parts as part of their bid to enter the World Trade Organisation. Furthermore, the deal required GM to source 40% of its components in China, rising to 80% by the third year. This, combined with China's underdeveloped supply chain for car manufacturers, threatened cost and quality. Because labour costs were a small and decreasing part of the overall cost of car manufacturing, there were no real benefits to be gained from one of China's greatest strengths, its supply of labour. After the deal was signed the overall market for cars in China stagnated, and sales of GM's high-quality model fell. Finally, although it seemed unlikely that the Chinese would offer a manufacturing licence to another car manufacturer, the withdrawal from the market of Peugeot meant that its licence became available, and Honda, one of GM's major competitors, won the bid.

GM took the long-term view, relying on the assumption that its business would grow and prosper as the Chinese economy, and demand, expanded. However, this case highlights the danger of external factors grouping together, threatening strategic decisions and major investments. It also illustrates the need for a practical understanding of the issues involved in major decisions.

Checklist: ensuring successful leadership decisions

Involve people in the decision-making process

Georges Clemenceau, a former French prime minister, said at the Versailles Conference in 1919:

> War is too serious a matter to be left to generals.

It is said, often insincerely, that people are the greatest resource of any organisation. However, when it comes to making and implementing decisions, it is people who largely determine success or failure. It is crucial, therefore, that employees are well managed, that their potential and ideas are exploited, and that they are motivated and committed.

Be honest and ethical
A business should demonstrate its honesty and integrity to both the outside world and its own employees. Decisions that lack integrity are unlikely to succeed and are likely to be damaging. Dishonesty leads to difficult decisions becoming worse or harder to make, and it may become impossible to make or implement future decisions as people's trust and respect diminish.

Understand that decisions set precedents
Decisions can set precedents that may be useful or a hindrance to decision-makers in the future. Consider not only whether a decision does set a precedent, but also whether the methods chosen for its implementation establish expectations for the future. Precedents can be useful in showing others how to make decisions, solve problems and manage in general. However, they may also establish bad practices as standard.

Show consistency and support
A characteristic of successful decision-makers is their commitment and enthusiasm. These virtues usually engender support as people generally respond well to the infectious nature of enthusiasm, provided it is not overwhelming or inappropriate. People also like to help, and enthusiasm often provides an opening for help and support to be offered.

Effectively implement decisions
Decisions can seem wonderful when considered in an office or a boardroom. However, there are three important points to remember:

- What matters is how the decision will work, even whether it can work. If a decision is not practical, it is doomed.
- To be practical, the decision must be dynamic. It must be flexible enough to take account of changing circumstances.
- Strategic decisions often need a patient, determined approach. It is what the decision sets out to achieve that matters rather than the decision itself. The decision is just a milestone on the way to the objective.

Be methodical
The taking and implementation of major decisions must be planned carefully and methodically. Planning and monitoring will help ensure that the right action is taken at the right time and will prevent problems building up. A methodical approach will also enable each stage to be completed before the next one starts. A too casual, too rushed or too unfocused approach is likely to produce an unsatisfactory result.

Stay positive and keep a sense of humour
Even in the face of adversity, it helps to maintain a "can-do" attitude. This is not to say that decisions should be treated lightly, but a positive mental attitude is an important source of strength and advantage. Behaviours to avoid in decision-making include procrastination or panic. Instead, adopting a calm, positive and appropriate approach that displays the right qualities at the right moment (such as urgency, caution, toughness and flexibility) increases the likelihood of success considerably. Always face up to problems. Never ignore them in the hope that they will go away.

Flying high: leadership essentials

The value of strong leadership is well known, but the qualities that matter most are perhaps less obvious. Jean-Cyril Spinetta, chairman and CEO of Air France, highlights several qualities.

First, value people. As Spinetta argues:

> If you do not like people, do another job. Understanding, motivating, mobilising and communicating with people are essential, and this is especially true in a service business such as an airline. The leader needs to uncover people's talents. The next quality is to reduce costs and be competitive, but also be sure that people understand the strategy. If people are unhappy or angry then the company suffers.

During times of concern over the quality of financial accounts and boardroom integrity, the importance of strong leadership is clear. As Spinetta advocates:

> Try to be transparent, clear and truthful. Even when it is difficult, and above all when it is difficult.

Developing a personal decision-making style

To ensure that your decision-making is effective, it can help to step back from the process and consider your typical approach. Where are the strengths and weaknesses in the approach? What action is needed to improve and develop skills and abilities in this area? In particular, reflect on each stage in the decision-making process and decide where skills might be enhanced.

This means knowing when a decision can be made independently and when support is needed from others. It also means knowing, for example, when to trust your instincts, when to gain further information and when to involve other people. Many other elements are significant: for example, when to apply principle and when to be pragmatic; when to compromise and when to be single-minded; when to be innovative and to challenge; when to conform; and above all, a sense of when a decision will succeed and when it will fail.

Through such an analysis the quality of decisions should improve, and there should also be more consistency, making it easier for others to understand and emulate them. Furthermore, developing a clear and con-sistent approach to decision-making provides a fallback position, so that when pressure and/or complexity increase or urgency escalates, there is a reliable, tried-and-tested approach to fall back on, honed during less stressful or critical times. To misquote Kipling: if you can keep your head while about you others are losing theirs, it is just possible you haven't grasped the situation.

However, there is no escape: the role of the strategic decision-maker is a pressured and lonely one, often with lingering uncertainty as an occupational hazard as the decision plays out. Developing personal strategies to handle this pressure is important, but ultimately, delivering decisions that achieve success is immensely rewarding. It is certainly worth remembering the words of Marie Curie, a particularly pressured, unconventional but effective decision-maker:

> *One never notices what has been done, one can only see what remains to be done.*

NOTES AND REFERENCES

1 Social, cultural and commercial forces

1 Handy, C., *The Empty Raincoat: Making Sense of the Future*, Random House, 1995 (published in the United States by Harvard Business School Press as *The Age of Paradox*).

2 Semler, R., *Maverick!*, Arrow, 1994.

3 Kaplan, R. and Norton, D., *The Balanced Scorecard: Translating Strategy into Action*, Harvard Business School Press, 1996.

4 Marchand, D.A., Kettinger, W.J. and Rollins, J., *Making the Invisible Visible*, John Wiley & Sons, 2001.

5 The US Small Business Administration published these figures in 1995, the last year for which reliable figures are available. Since then, the cost is estimated to have increased by a further 12%.

6 Drucker, P., "They're Not Employees, They're People", *Harvard Business Review*, February 2002.

7 Stewart, T.A., *Intellectual Capital*, Doubleday, 1997.

8 Drucker, P., *The Age of Discontinuity*, Harper and Row, 1969.

9 For further information, see Edvinsson, L. and Malone, M., *Intellectual Capital: Realising Your Company's True Value by Finding its Hidden Brainpower*, HarperBusiness, 1997.

10 Peters, T. and Waterman, R., *In Search of Excellence*, Harper and Row, 1982.

11 Naisbitt, J., *Global Paradox: the bigger the global economy, the more powerful its smallest players*, Simon and Schuster, 1995.

12 "Special Report: Diasporas", *The Economist*, January 4th 2003.

13 Globalisation statistics are provided by the Economist Intelligence Unit. For further information, see www.eiu.com, and also the Economist Intelligence Unit's *World Competitiveness Yearbook*.

14 This example and the broader issues it raises are expertly explored in Read, C., Ross, J., Dunleavy, J., Schulman, D. and Bramante. J., *eCFO: sustaining value in the corporation*, John Wiley & Sons, 2001.

15 Marchand, D.A. (ed.), *Competing with Information: A manager's guide to creating business value with information content*, John Wiley & Sons, 1999.

16 Marchand *et al.*, *Making the Invisible Visible*.

17 Drucker, P., *Management Challenges for the Twenty-First Century*, Butterworth-Heinemann, 1999.

18 Pearce, F., "Mamma Mia", *New Scientist*, July 20th 2002.

19 Kellaway, L., "Boardroom Styles", *The World in 2003, The Economist*, 2003.

2 Ideas at work

1   Farnham, A., "The man who changed work forever", *Fortune*, July 21st 1997.
2   Written by Frederick Taylor in 1911 in *The Principles of Scientific Management*. For a more recent analysis, see Taylor, F., *Scientific Management*, Harper and Row, 1948.
3   Ansoff, I., *Corporate Strategy*, McGraw-Hill, 1965.
4   Hamel, G. and Prahalad, C.K., *Competing for the Future*, Harvard Business School Press, 1994.
5   Peters and Waterman, *In Search of Excellence*.
6   Senge, P., *The Fifth Discipline: The Art and Practice of the Learning Organisation*, Doubleday, 1991.
7   Porter, M., "Strategy and the Internet", *Harvard Business Review*, March 2001.
8   Hamilton, S., "Information and the Management of Risk", in Marchand, D.A. (ed.), *Competing with Information: A Manager's Guide to Creating Business Value with Information Content*, John Wiley & Sons, 1999.
9   Hamilton, "Information and the Management of Risk".
10 Kaplan and Norton, *The Balanced Scorecard*.

3 Pitfalls

1   Hammond, J.S., Keeney, R.L. and Raiffa, H., "The Hidden Traps in Decision-making", *Harvard Business Review*, September–October 1998.
2   Harvey, J.B., "The Abilene Paradox: The Management of Agreement", *Journal of Organisational Dynamics*, 1974.
3   Grinyer, P., Mayes, D. and McKiernan, P., *Sharpbenders: The Secrets of Unleashing Corporate Potential*, Blackwell, 1989.
4   De Geus, A., "Planning as Learning", *Harvard Business Review*, Vol. 66, No. 2, 1988, pp. 70–74.
5   Van der Heijden, K., *Scenarios: The Art of Strategic Conversation*, John Wiley & Sons, 1996.

4 Rational or intuitive? Frameworks for decision-making

1   Drucker, P., "The Effective Decision", *Harvard Business Review*, January–February 1967.
2   Drucker, "The Effective Decision".
3   Quoted in Hayashi, A.M., "When to Trust Your Gut", *Harvard Business Review*, February 2001.
4   Hayashi, "When to Trust Your Gut".

5 Making strategic decisions

1 Apter, M.J. (ed.), *Motivational Styles in Everyday Life: A Guide to Reversal Theory*, American Psychological Association, Washington DC, 2001. This is a comprehensive review of the research undertaken on reversal theory as well as its applications. It also provides a complete and definitive statement of the theory.

2 Apter, M.J. (ed.), *Motivational Styles in Everyday Life*.

6 Scenario thinking

1 Porter, M., *Competitive Advantage: Creating and Sustaining Superior Performance*, Free Press, 1998.

2 Van der Heijden, K., *The Sixth Sense*, John Wiley & Sons, 2002.

3 Van der Heijden, *Scenarios*.

8 Competitive strategy

1 Benezra, K., "Chasing Sergio: how Sergio Zyman picked himself up after the new Coke debacle and became keeper of the brand equity flame at Coca-Cola", *Brandweek*, Vol. 39, March 30th 1998, p. 30.

2 Sean Meehan, a professor at IMD in Lausanne, one of the world's leading authorities on marketing dynamics and market sensing, provides this definition. See Meehan, S., "Leveraging Market Sensing to Create Competitive Advantage", in Marchand (ed.), *Competing with Information*.

9 Customer focus

1 Meehan, S., "Leveraging Market Sensing to Create Competitive Advantage".

10 Knowledge and information

1 Marchand *et al.*, *Making the Invisible Visible*. Marchand has established his own business, enterpriseIQ, to commercialise this research and has developed a suite of diagnostic tools for analysing organisational effectiveness in employing information to improve performance.

2 For further details, see "The Truth about CRM", *CIO Magazine*, May 1st 2001.

3 These examples appeared in Marchand, D., "How Effective is Your Company at Using Information?", *European Business Forum*, Winter 2001.

4 See Garvin, D.A., "Building a Learning Organisation", *Harvard*

Business Review, July–August 1993.

5   The cycle of learning, also known as Kolb's learning cycle, was developed by David Kolb, and appeared in Kolb, D., *Experiential Learning as a Source of Learning and Development*, Prentice Hall, 1984.

6   Van der Heijden, *Scenarios*.

7   Mintzberg, H., *The Rise and Fall of Strategic Planning*, Free Press, 1994.

11   Managing finance and risk

1   This concept was expertly outlined by Michael Porter in *Competitive Strategy: Techniques for Analysing Industries and Competitors*, Free Press, 1980.

2   There are many excellent books detailing the financial techniques that can be applied by non-financial managers for decision-making. See, for example, Harrison, J., *Finance for the Non-Financial Manager*, HarperCollins, 1989.

3   A guide to overcoming the fear of risk is provided in Kourdi, J. and Carter, S., *The Road to Audacity*, Palgrave Macmillan, 2003.

12   Sales, marketing and brand management decisions

1   This resource view is the essence of systems analysis and is discussed in depth by Kim Warren, a professor at London Business School. See Warren, K., *Competitive Strategy Dynamics*, John Wiley & Sons, 2002.

2   Survey results reported on www.silicon.com.

13   Leadership

1   Singh, S., *Fermat's Last Theorem*, Fourth Estate, 1997.

2   Dennett, D.C., *How Things Are*, Weidenfeld & Nicolson, 1995.

3   Barbour, J., *The End of Time*, Weidenfeld & Nicolson, 1999.

INDEX